EMPOWER THE WARRIOR *Within*

10 STEPS TO TRANSFORM YOUR BREAKUP INTO YOUR GREATEST BREAKTHROUGH

VANESSA GOANS

Empower The Warrior Within:
10 Steps to Transform Your Breakup into Your Greatest Breakthrough

Note: This book is intended to be used as an informative guide for those who have been through a breakup and does not in any way replace the advice from doctors, therapists, and other health care professionals. The author and publisher specifically disclaim any liability directly or indirectly stemming from the use of this book.

MANHATTAN
BOOK GROUP

Published by Manhattan Book Group, an imprint of MindStir Media, LLC
447 Broadway | 2nd Floor #354 | New York, NY 10013 | USA
212-634-7677 | www.manhattanbookgroup.com

Printed in the United States of America
ISBN: (paperback): 978-1-7376522-0-5
ISBN (eBook): 978-1-7376522-1-2

DEDICATION

To all those who have experienced the emotional pain of abandonment after a sudden breakup.

May you find:

Encouragement and comfort

Love and peace

Healing and hope

Laughter

And a better you.

TABLE OF CONTENTS

ACKNOWLEDGEMENTS

Though life is full of tragedies and pain, there is still love. For recognizing this truth I am eternally grateful. It is impossible to write a book alone. I cannot begin to mention the numerous individuals who have helped me fulfill my dream of writing this book. I want to extend my heartfelt gratitude to the following people who contributed and believed in making this book possible:

My family, friends, mentors, professors, and first readers for your unwavering support. Steve Harrison and his team for sharing their publishing experience. Special thanks to my book coach Cristina Smith, and Geoffrey Berwind for their expert feedback and guidance. Jack Canfield and Patty Aubrey for reigniting my desire to self-publish and motivating me to finish my book. Jack Tuckner, Deborah O'Rell, Beverly Kitson-Solomon, Patricia Ann Russell, and Sandra Russell-Flowers for giving me their time and support when I needed it most.

I also couldn't publish on time without J.J. Hebert

and his team, including editor Juli Burgett and book manager Jen McNabney. Appreciate the assistance of Stephen Cardone and Kemi Kamugisha who organized my headshot. Finally, to my readers, I say thank you, because through your own difficult experiences you teach the world, and me, that we are strong enough to meet any challenge life may put upon us. May the words in this book empower you to find healing and hope to rise above your emotional pain to achieve your vision of a successful life.

MY STORY

Like snowflakes and fingerprints, there are no carbon copies of you.

This book contains stories of my childhood and relationship experiences along with a step-by-step guide to help you realize there is light at the end of a painful breakup. If I could rise above dysfunction and heal from my breakup, so can you. The process of healing requires work but the rewards at the end of the journey are endless and surely worth the effort.

IF I HAD TO SAY one word that describes my childhood, I'd say "bittersweet." Were there more good times than bad or bad times than good? I couldn't begin to tell. But bad experiences linger like that obnoxious garlic smell that lodges on your breath, despite persistent efforts to erase its scent. While I worked hard over the years to remove those stains of bad experiences growing up, the memories still linger. The good that forever remains with me are those solo escapes I took to the bamboo patches at my great-grandmother's house to watch the metamorphosis of butterflies.

Where the woods were the thickest, I would rest under the canopy of trees in full bloom. Watching caterpillars turning into butterflies was one of the most fascinating transformations I've ever witnessed. It mesmerized me then and imprinted a lasting impression in my mind about the importance of change and also of closure. Minutes turned into hours as I studied the ladybugs traversing nonchalantly, sashaying in their Sunday best on blades of grass, as butterflies danced to the chorus of insects coming to life. The surroundings serenaded me to a drowsy stupor as the sun played peekaboo with me through the shade. Those moments were my definition of happiness.

On one of those days, I remember reaching out to touch the wings of a butterfly with the innocent intention of admiring its beauty. But, to my horror, I realized that I had taken its life instead. It was a cheap lesson for me, but an expensive one for the insect, of how fragile life could be. It was a lesson of how easily your wings can be clipped and life taken away, denying you the goals you had hoped to achieve. This event made me ponder about my purpose and why I was brought into this world. Soon, I lapsed back into my usual daydream of traveling the globe, plotting my escape.

It was in those moments that I thought about why

my family was dysfunctional. I knew that something was not working quite right within my nuclear family that made me associate being at my mother's house with bad experiences and my great-grandmother's house with good experiences. At my mother's house, I faced a constant barrage of drama; in my great-grandmother's house, I found peace and refuge.

Throughout elementary school, I was caught in the crossfire of my parents' messy divorce. Life in our household felt like the reenactment of an intense conflict on a battlefield, where I had to somersault out of the line of fire to hide in a bunker until it was safe to come out from cover. Picking up the empty shell cases of my parents' broken relationship seemed like a never-ending and senseless exercise in patriotic duty to preserve the family name. My mother had entered an abusive relationship and stayed in it for what she rationalized as a necessity for the sake of her children. Although my mother spent a lifetime hiding the physical pain of abuse, to me she seemed emotionally wounded, buried under unfulfilled dreams, and scarred like that frightened butterfly that had never tested its wings in flight. Instead, there she sat, allowing her husband to clip her fragile wings.

I recognize now that my mother did what she deemed was her best to raise us. I spent most of my time away at my great-grandmother's house to avoid my mother's passiveness and the endless nightmares of a father coming into the house like a Goliath to create mayhem only to vanish again. There, I would daydream and promise myself to do better. My great-grandmother, affectionately known as Granny, kept those daydreams alive and saved me from feeling completely abandoned.

A chubby woman with a lap like pillows, she had a wild mixture of curly and straight hair, was curvaceously built, and was full of ancestral wisdom. She was a reservoir of herbal medicine handed down by word of mouth for generations. The slightest hint of congestion would open the floodgates of cures. It was not uncommon to get rubbed down with white rum mixed with soft candle wax during the rainy season. Or, in some cases, she would heat aloe vera on the stovetop then slap the concoction against your skin while still sizzling to cure some sort of foot injury. Strangely enough, those home remedies from her arsenal of herbs did work.

Granny just seemed to know how to fix everything, from ailments to mending your clothes when the seams came undone. I regarded her as a strong, deeply religious woman, and we all revered her as the family's matriarch. She had strong convictions of family, hard work, and commitment, having raised nine children single-handedly after two failed relationships. Those breakups didn't seem to bother her as she still carried on with life. She didn't inherit wealth and had to work for everything she had, so losing relationships with men didn't seem to matter. But family did.

In a peculiar way, Granny became the person I could have girl-talk with about love, life, marriage, divorce, abandonment, and men. She never scolded me for asking questions way beyond my years or labelled me as the nosey kid who always tried to get involved in adult business. After answering even the most pointed questions about marriage, she would always say with a smile, "Don't let disappointments in life reduce you to ruin, don't worry about anything. Go, you will do good."

I was around twelve years old when Granny died, and my comfort zone died with her. Although I could no longer have any girl-talk with her about relationships, she left behind valuable lessons about love and life. To me, she was a *warrior*. The warrior within her made it possible to raise nine children as a single parent. The warrior within her gave her the strength to build her own house. The warrior within her didn't allow breakups to break or paralyze her. Instead, she courageously worked hard to live a successful life using the knowledge she had available at the time. Whether she was emotionally wounded or not from the breakups she experienced, she just kept going.

Those fond memories of my Granny later became a guiding compass of what to do and what not to do when entering or leaving relationships. So, in 2004, when I fell in love and got married, I thought I'd learned everything I needed to learn from Granny's experiences. I thought I had ended the curse of generational divorce. I thought my wedding day was the beginning of a new chapter, and I would have my happily ever after.

Little did I know that getting married was not just a new stage of learning but also the beginning of my own transformation.

INTRODUCTION

Up until March 27, 2015, I would describe my marriage as blissful. After a fairytale proposal and wedding, we enjoyed what I thought was a healthy, happy relationship. Our interests were similar in many respects. We finished each other's sentences, as some would say. As cliché as this may sound, the saying was true. We were intertwined in our purpose, chemistry, goals, dreams, and expectations. We shared our darkest secrets and reached the pinnacle of trust and comfort required for the foundation of any successful relationship.

Enjoying similar interests, values, mutual friends, and family kinship were delightful—it was the bedrock of security that I expected to achieve in marriage which was deficient in my own upbringing. We seemed to weather even the most challenging financial and emotional times, strongly united as one unit pressing forward towards our goals for a better future together.

We had our disagreements like most healthy relationships throughout the two years of dating and many years married, but we avoided bitter fights, resentments, and uncompromising debates. Life and marriage, to us, were nothing but euphoric love. At least so I thought. At times, even ten years into our marriage, I would jokingly say to curious friends, echoing his sentiments, "We are still on our honeymoon." It certainly felt like a honeymoon throughout the time we were together. No sign of trouble—nothing visible in "Pandora's Box." I really believed my marriage could withstand the test of time and could not possibly become a part of those common divorce stories that I read about. However, in the spring of 2015, as I began to finalize plans for our annual vacation, my world started shifting on its axis.

March was almost over. I spent one of many college spring breaks in an uneventful fashion, juggling the responsibilities of running a household, working a full-time job, and studying engineering for finals. As I fantasized about our vacation plans to visit Aruba on our 11th year honeymoon, I seemed to have made it to my destination in record time, driving with my usual excitement to see my husband after a long workday. Despite my elation, as he opened the door, a hush seemed to overtake the atmosphere in the car as he sat. For sure, I thought he must have had a really bad day at work since this sudden silent treatment was very new to me. I attempted to canvass for dialogue about our upcoming vacation just weeks away but that didn't work to break the ice.

Perplexed by his apathy, I pointedly asked, "Honey, what's wrong, why aren't you speaking?"

He responded with a strange indifference, "I've just been feeling depressed lately."

Granted, while I strived to empathize and sympathize with the depression self-diagnosis, I did not quite buy the whitewashed response. Deep inside my heart, I knew something was terribly wrong. For your talkative best friend to suddenly be reduced to silence would have to take some sort of life-altering event. My intuition needed an answer, so after a silent ride home, as I parked in the driveway, I reassured him he could talk to me about anything. With the goal of understanding the sudden shift in our communication, I requested that he not alienate me. I tried to assure him that if something was wrong, we had been in a relationship long enough for him to let me know the barrier that was standing at the gate of our communication. As I gently stroked his shoulder, I asked again, "Is there another reason you are suddenly not speaking with me at all?"

He then gestured his body away from my touch and responded with even more indifference, in one abrupt sentence, "We will talk inside."

The astonishing behavior escalated to a whole new level as I came inside the house and sat beside him to talk about what was bothering him. Without making eye contact and removing himself from the proximity of my touch, he bluntly said, "We have grown apart. I have developed feelings for someone at work and these feelings I have for her I cannot shake."

Dumbfounded, I tried to process what he was saying as he continued broadcasting his feelings for another woman. The words seemed to come out of his mouth in slow motion as I envisioned he had transformed into a stranger who was philosophizing about the end of a marriage he knew nothing about. At the time, it seemed like my husband was an apparition of the man I once knew.

Then it was over. My mind went completely blank. At that moment, I thought my life had ended from the impact of what I perceived was a semi-truck that just landed a blow to the center of my chest. It was all a blur, but in a split second, I was facing what seemed like the exhalation of my last breath. In the backdrop of his voice, my mind jolted back to our wedding day, to happier times, past experiences, to places we've been and those we've yet to discover.

I felt I was dreaming, my past rising up to meet me through a foggy glass window as I watched people fine dining while soft violins serenaded in the background. Though the scene was clouded and frozen in time, as I wiped the fog off the glass with frozen fingers, I saw myself sitting at one of the tables; beautiful, happy, decked in white next to my husband. I could smell the fresh lilies blooming on the table and hear my whispers in his ears fading into the chattering voices and clanking of cutlery. Before I could process the scenery, I got whisked away in his arms through heavy doors leading to another dimension of the place.

As I continued to be lost in the trance of my past, those random thoughts seemed strange to me, because through those doors was the glare of a blinding light. Headlights I didn't see coming until they were right in front of me. The light engulfed me and left me with no time to react. My hands reached in front of me to protect myself from the impact of what was about to hit me, but I only collected air. Then it happened. The collision was so severe, I could hear my bones crackle and surrender under the force of the vehicle that came to a screeching halt. The driver didn't seem to realize I was a woman he used to know. In his oblivion, he drove on his way, leaving me only to inhale the exhaust from whatever chariot he was riding. I thought by now I would hear sirens wailing in the distance, but there was only silence, as I tasted my blood that had just spilled on the icy roadway. As the blinding light disappeared, it became more apparent I was not hit by a stranger but by my own husband in our very own living room.

As I came back to reality, I discerned he was still rambling. My dissociated mind drifted in and out of confusion and my body became paralyzed, as I tried to contain the commotion in my heart that would be followed by a shattered marriage. My life flashed before me as my brain tried to process the madness I was listening to that thrust my world into turmoil. Indeed, it certainly felt like I was literally hit by a semi-truck I didn't see coming as I stood looking at my life through a foggy glass window. The memories of our wedding day and our history together collided with his words like burning arrows shot through the air and piercing through my heart, shattering it into a million pieces. It seemed as if I was a bystander watching his declarations become entangled in a wreckage of what was once our happy marriage.

As he continued speaking, I sat peacefully as my body braced for turbulence, listening to his calm explanations of lunch dates at work, text messages, and times spent together getting to know this other woman better. His narrative was callous, brutal, without remorse, and with no recognition of the magnitude of emotional damage he was inflicting on me, us, or the history we shared. His unreasonable disclosure almost seemed as though he was expecting me to fall to my knees and beg for his love or give my concurrence to wish him eternal happiness for his new budding relationship. The entire event felt like a bad dream or a cruel joke. Whatever the case, I was not amused!

Ultimately, the upshot message of this revelation was just like flipping off a light switch to our relationship. The man I loved, and who I thought loved me back, wanted to abruptly end our marriage after going on some lunch dates with a coworker. The trust, happiness, and bedrock of comfort we had built, suddenly, in one night, was gone like mist in the wind. Reeling from the total devastation that night, I remembered the voice of my Granny saying, "Don't let disappointments in life reduce you to ruin, don't worry about anything. Go, you will do good!"

Those thoughts were the only sanity check I remembered at the time. Exhausted, shocked and in total upheaval, I tabled the discussion and went to bed. At the moment, I was still hoping that what I heard was a man who had a rough day and who had developed some unexplained insanity overnight.

As the morning broke, I turned lazily towards my husband's side of the bed as the sun peeked through the curtain and danced around the room. Though that new day was beautiful, only the sun was dancing in my household. The emptiness that replaced the butterflies in my stomach that Saturday morning was one experience I would not soon forget. That feeling tortured me. For the first time in all the years of being married, my husband's side of the bed remained unruffled as he'd slept on the couch overnight.

I descended the stairs to the living room and entered the scene of a man I once knew sitting stoically, staring at the television as if hypnotized. As I broke his stare, hoping he would confirm that his revelations the night before were only a dream, he instead validated that his feelings for the other woman were real. Our marriage, for the first time I could recall, was approaching shipwreck and I was unable to save it. Not only was I not able to save my marriage, but I was also silenced. The decision to end the relationship seemed like it was already made and there were no discussions allowed about the matter.

I must admit, I surprised myself as I calmly reasoned with him to take the necessary steps to repair our marriage before it became irretrievably broken. His response was life-changing and the first time I heard words of discontent from him. From his perspective we were already living separate lives, he had feelings for someone else, he was not open to marriage counseling, and it was too late to repair our marriage.

In other words, without warning or the courtesy of an opportunity to salvage what we were about to lose, I had no say in the matter. The decision to separate and end the marriage was already unilaterally made. I just had to accept the "mother of all bombs" that just fell in my lap, and I was left in the bloodbath to deal with the aftershock. To be robbed so viciously of closure without the opportunity to process the emotional damage of the sudden end to our marriage took every fiber in me not to lash out.

After my breakup I was in agonizing pain, riding what felt like a rollercoaster of complex emotional feelings. I certainly didn't feel like a warrior, but I really needed advice from one. If you've similarly experienced the devastating end of a romantic relationship, know that it is possible to turn the painful loss into valuable lessons and success beyond what you'd ever imagined. You can thrive and go on to live a successful life after a breakup. This book will give you the evidence, stories, and tools you can use to achieve this success. The journey I travelled to heal from the emotional damage of sudden abandonment after a breakup is narrated step by step in each chapter of this book which will help you to:

Step 1 - Overcome the initial shock of the breakup.
Step 2 - Let go of anger.
Step 3 - Overcome denial.
Step 4 - Heal from blame.
Step 5 - Cope with financial loss.
Step 6 - Practice the art of gratitude.
Step 7 - Learn to forgive.
Step 8 - Take control of your life.
Step 9 - Find closure.
Step 10 - Write your narrative to live your best life.

These ten steps helped me to progressively become whole again. This book will also help you find happiness while traversing your trials and personal struggles after the abrupt ending to your relationship. Although the journey may be quite a challenge, you must know that the real struggle is inside you. When those struggles confront you, do not retreat or let these challenges break you. You must keep going no matter how painful the loss of love and be ready to accept the best treasures life has in store for you. Most importantly, know that there is a warrior within you waiting to be trained to conquer your greatest fears; the devastation of a breakup does not define who you are and who you can become.

HOW TO READ THIS BOOK

THE INTENT OF THIS BOOK is to help you get through your breakup or divorce and use the experience as a launching pad towards achieving your own success. The process of attaining this personal breakthrough to have the life you deserve is outlined in each chapter. This book will help you do the self-examination required to determine if you are still stuck in any of the stages of grief. I suggest you start with a pen or highlighter to mark the areas in the book that resonate with you as you continue reading. You may revisit sections of the book to acknowledge areas where you believe you've already achieved emotional completeness. Most importantly, Chapters 1-4 contain journal commentaries related to your breakup. After completing the last page of these four chapters, whenever you feel like you have conquered the stages of shock, anger, denial, or blame, discard the page, and let it all go.

CHAPTER 1

OVERCOMING THE INITIAL SHOCK

Fear is but a shadow.
Like mist it dissipates as we navigate through it.

FOR THOSE WHO HAVE BEEN through a breakup or those currently going through one, the sudden ending of a once happy relationship can be a shocking and frightening experience. The initial stages of grief are the hardest parts of the recovery process as you try to work through each step of your emotional pain. Your breakup may cause you to question everything and leave you wondering if you can trust or even date again. It may leave you feeling afraid for your financial future, filled with sorrow, and overwhelmed at the thought of putting your life back together while navigating through the lengthy divorce process if married.

Your self-confidence may be wounded because the person you love suddenly rejected you, emotionally switched off from the relationship, and hurt you in some unimaginable ways. If you experienced physical abuse in the relationship, you might wonder how to get real help to heal both your physical and emotional wounds.

Your emotions can become jumbled, and you may feel helpless, angry, defeated, insecure, blindsided, and shaken. Every task may seem difficult, and a way out from the emotional darkness of losing love may seem impossible to overcome. As you try to sift through the ashes of the ruined relationship, you go through the motions of daily living. Still traumatized about the breakup, you may be wondering why it ended, how it ended, and when your pain will subside. The embarrassment and humiliation of letting family, friends, and children know the relationship fell apart can be excruciating. People handle the shocking experience of a breakup in different ways but the rollercoaster of emotions can collectively feel the same. Simply put, breakups really hurt.

The sudden emotional abandonment by the person you sincerely love defies all logic and requires courage by the one affected in the aftermath of this type of abuse. It is the initial shock and the question of why that has most people gasping for air and trying to make sense of the nonsense, to find the flaw that caused the relationship to disintegrate. If you are going through a recent breakup, you are probably scrambling to find books, anyone, or anything to help you deal with the fall out of abandonment.

While there are many publications that address separation or divorce and the aftereffects, there are still few tools available that can prepare you to be resilient while going through a painful and sudden breakup. Most resources on breakups categorize divorce, marital complications, and abandonment as the same experiences. Still few people understand that there is a vast difference between sudden abandonment and the other forms of relationship breakups.

Abandonment is much more complicated than a mutual decision by both parties to divorce. Often, sudden abandonment leaves complex wounds that are very difficult to heal, and there is not enough support or resources to deal with the emotional impact of sudden abandonment. It was this scarcity of information about sudden abandonment that became the catalyst behind me finding a way to devise my own roadmap to healing. At first the shock of the sudden ending of your relationship may be very hard to accept. I'm sure you are anxious to have your life back to some sort of normalcy again. However, in the middle of this emotionally charged crisis there is much to learn, grow, and evolve from. To transform the initial shock of the breakup into your greatest breakthrough, you must work hard to redirect the focus of healing to yourself. How does one achieve this healing?

ACKNOWLEDGE YOUR REACTIONS ARE NATURAL

When a person sustains a life-threatening injury, the body goes through a state of shock. This protective mechanism of the body keeps you from feeling overwhelmed until the mind can process and begin to assess the damage you've sustained. Even the best warriors sometimes get wounded. But after the initial shock of an injury, instead of losing control over a stressful situation, a wounded warrior may calmly access the damage in order to mitigate pain and preserve life. In a similar way, the emotional wounds you've suffered from your breakup require that you give attention to yourself and consider how you will overcome your fears to heal from your internal injuries. As the opening quote highlighted, fear is only a shadow and will vanish like mist once you take the steps to navigate through it.

Acknowledge that your feelings of shock, fear, and confusion over the ending of the relationship are natural reactions to the situation. If you are feeling like you are about to implode with stress, take action to speak with someone you trust about your feelings and practice self-care so you can achieve some level of internal peace while you go through the stages of grief. Remaining calm may not be on your top list of actions to take during an emotional crisis, but it is one of the best ways you can maintain mental clarity and rational thinking.

It may be quite tempting to slash your ex's car tires, vandalize his or her belongings, or carry out some other vengeful act. But remember, irrational thoughts, lashing out, and other negative actions may result in some unpleasant consequences for you. Understandably, remaining calm and having a rational discussion with the person you love after that individual inflicted such unimaginable emotional pain may seem farfetched. However, speaking and acting rationally during a painful situation is possible.

Reflections

As impossible as my situation felt at the time of my breakup, I was able to prepare dinner as usual, wash his clothes, and talk with civility to my husband while living with him in the same household for thirty days after his confessions. Living with my husband for this period of time did not get me any reasonable answers as to why I was being abandoned but it certainly gave me power over a situation where I initially felt powerless. In the final analysis, I had the strength to wave goodbye to him in the driveway as he disappeared in a fog to begin the new life he decided to live. Remaining calm and thinking rationally also made it possible to finish college finals and travel alone to Aruba for "my" 11th year anniversary instead of "ours," to celebrate the new single life that was forced upon me. It certainly was not easy at the time. But this self-care trip, massages on the beach, self-reflections, spiritual meditations, swimming exercises, and mental focus on myself saved me.

Thinking rationally while facing a stressful situation allows you to employ a regimen that will nourish your body and mind. Your routine of self-care does not have to cost a substantial amount of money. Some ways you can deal with breakup stress are: eat healthy nutritious foods, get sufficient sleep, develop an exercise routine, take a walk in nature at a local park to reflect on positive things about yourself, enjoy a spa day, have a "ME" day (that is, a day just for you to recharge). Whatever it takes, do what you can to take care of yourself. Taking care of yourself may be the last thing on your mind but it should be the first.

START A JOURNAL

Starting a journal is an important part of the healing process from the initial shock of a breakup. It transfers the shock and pain out of your mind and onto paper. Keeping a daily journal allows you to track the progress you've made throughout the healing process and is an essential tool to help you maintain mental clarity. Since writing a journal is a conversation with yourself, you can achieve a similar comfort writing to yourself as you would talking with a friend about the emotional impact of the breakup. Write about your heartbreak, frustrations, anger, fears, insecurities, anxieties, or anything that comes to mind. Equally important, as you write down all the negative things you feel about the breakup, replace those with positive thoughts. For instance:

SHOCK can be written negatively as: Shame, Humiliation, Obsession, Chaos and Kainotophobia (fear of change),

or

SHOCK can be written positively as: Smart, Hopeful, Optimistic, Courageous and Kind.

Journaling is a powerful mental health management tool. It can help you keep perspective while dealing with stressors in your life, and evoke the self-introspection needed to manage or achieve emotional balance. The more you write positive thoughts about yourself, the more you will reinforce positive thoughts in your mind. Your journal becomes part of your personal history and experience that you can learn from. Granted, at first you may write more about your negative experiences with your ex, but over time you may gradually begin to see a pattern develop where you start writing more positive things about yourself.

Your evolution, self-awareness, and personal development become more pronounced as the shock and pain from the breakup dissipates. At one point in my journal, I wrote the word *enough*. This was the day I discovered it was time to move on and stop dwelling on negative thoughts stemming from the breakup. That day of healing will take time, but it will also come for you, when you are ready to do the work to heal and you've had enough of wasting precious energy thinking about the negative details of your breakup.

STAY IN MOTION

After a breakup, it takes courage to stay connected with others. The isolation and emptiness after a relationship ends can be a tough void to fill, especially during special anniversaries and holiday occasions. Often, when you break up you may lose not only your mate but also relationships with in-laws, family, and mutual friends. Some people may have personal opinions about your breakup and others may be wrapped up in their own lives too much to care about yours one way or the other. Either way, it can be a very solitary feeling after a breakup since no one can truly understand the depth of your emotional suffering.

Regardless of how lonely you may feel, stay in motion. Connect with people who share a genuine interest in your well-being. Develop a support network to help you through this initial stage of shock. Close family members, friends, spiritual advisors, therapists, divorce support groups, and other professionals can all be supportive and really help you survive the aftermath of a breakup. Feed your mind with wholesome thoughts by reading motivational books and replacing negative thinking with positive affirmations. Perhaps joining a dance group, gym, social club, or learning new hobbies and skills to repair your living space will help you to stay in motion. I remember painting the entire house all by myself, decluttering and rearranging my living space to create my own sanctuary. That mini home makeover gave me a sense of accomplishment and created a calm atmosphere to do the necessary work to heal myself.

LEARN FROM OTHERS

Warriors do not develop skills overnight on their own. They learn from others and take time out for training. Be patient with yourself. Accept the fact that healing and the grief process will take time. Find your inner strength by learning from the successes and mistakes of others. Think about other people who have been through divorce and how they handled this situation.

Reflections

I thought about my Granny and what advice she would give. I paraded her like a heroine in my mind after my breakup. I reflected on my life and the impact any unfinished self-development had on my subconscious. Did I somehow let the drama of my parents' dysfunctional life bleed into my own life? Was I about to let my husband clip my wings just like that butterfly from the bamboo patch? It was the thought that I could fail at the finish line at any given moment that both haunted and motivated me. The fear of failure became more frightening than fear of the work involved in succeeding after my relationship failed. Until this epiphany, it didn't occur to me that I could find a heroine hidden in the ashes within parts of my dysfunctional childhood. Thinking of certain aspects of her life woke up a warrior inside me.

Mentors and experiences from others may give you wisdom you can store in your own emotional reservoir. These mentors coupled with the right plan of action can help you to successfully conquer your emotional pain. Who are the warriors that you can learn from? Is it someone from your past, someone you read about, a teacher, a friend, a public figure, a doctor, a therapist? Is your warrior you? What success stories could you draw upon to give you clearer perspective that you can handle anything, including your breakup? How determined are you to accomplish your goals with or without your companion?

Goals and success can mean different things to each person. You will need to find ways to use the experiences from your warriors to fulfill your own level of empowerment. Whether you choose to empower yourself through education, culture, community activities or other means, you must decide how to tap into your inner warrior. As difficult as it may seem, facing the shock of your breakup and your inner pain instead of retreating is one of the most important keys to transformation. It is the first step to healing as you begin to recreate your new life to achieve your breakthrough and bravely conquer the next phase of healing, letting go of anger.

Four reminders to help you overcome shock:

1. HEAD - Warriors wear helmets to protect their brains. You must acknowledge your feelings of pain and grief are normal reactions. Protect your mind from depression and self-defeating thoughts by practicing self-care, setting up "ME" days, reading, spiritual meditation, and feeding your mind with positive thoughts.
2. CHEST - Warriors carry a shield to protect their vital organs. You must also protect your heart. Keep a journal to record everything: The injury to your broken heart, frustrations, anger, fears, insecurities, and anxieties. Write down all the positive things about your life. One day, as your heart begins to heal, you will have had enough of wasting energy thinking about your ex.
3. FEET - Warriors wear protective boots to keep moving. You also must stay in motion. Develop your support group and get involved with activities that will keep you motivated.
4. ARMOR - Even with the best armor warriors can get wounded, but they keep going. They make calm, calculated decisions despite fear and they never give up. Who can you learn from past or present that will empower you and refine your training to keep fighting and going after your goals?

These reminders will prepare your mind for dealing with the next critical step to healing, letting go of anger.

JOURNAL COMMENTARY

What shocked me most about my breakup was

____

____

When I was abandoned, I felt like

____

____

The phrases that resonated with me in this chapter

____

____

I find it difficult to let go because

____

____

After reading this chapter I realize

____

____

I accept the truth that I

____

____

Today I am not the victim but the victor because

____

When you feel like you have become the champion over your experience, when you feel like you have become your own warrior, immediately discard this page. Cut it into tiny pieces. Whatever you do, after you feel emotionally complete, just let it go.

CHAPTER 2

LETTING GO OF ANGER

Warning Signs

The trials on the road you are travelling will have warning signs and mirrors for you to see your own truth.

SUDDEN CHANGE CAN BE PAINFUL, and nothing can prepare you for the emotional impact of abandonment after a breakup. This type of change is unique to the individual, involves multiple steps towards healing, and can be extremely complex. The complexity of this change can be even more complicated if the failure of the relationship involves children caught in the crossfire. Parents going through difficult emotions from abandonment with one or more children after the sudden collapse of a relationship can be even more challenging. While parents deal with the new reality of divorce as an adult, the trauma of separation and divorce is greatly amplified for the children.

Remember, the way you choose to save yourself, your words, your actions, and your decisions will all be observed by your children, who will be taking mental notes. How you react to your breakup situation may become the generational footprint for your children to follow and shape the way they perceive both parents through their own lenses. Never would you want your actions to negatively impact your children to suffer the same emotional pain you may have to navigate as an adult throughout the divorce process. Since the disintegration of your relationship is in the spotlight, you must be able to look beyond the breakup, regardless of your own emotional struggles and avoid any uncontrolled angry bouts as you make timely decisions in the best interest of your future.

HEALTHY ANGER

While being angry over the way your relationship ended is an appropriate reaction, acting on your anger is not okay. Anger can either be expressed in a healthy or unhealthy way. Some people may express anger through violence which may have bad repercussions for the parties involved. Others may try to repress their anger only to have it manifest itself in other aspects of life such as road rage, lashing out at other people for no reason, or just being in a bad mood all the time. Instead of keeping your anger inside without expressing it or projecting unrestrained anger onto others, it is important to acknowledge your anger and find healthy ways to deal with it.

> Reflections
>
> After a solo trip just after my breakup, I returned home to multiple social media photos that showed my husband had quickly moved on to his new love interest. I was angry seeing him sashay with another woman within days of our breakup. Months later he had a change of heart and asked for a second chance to reconcile our relationship. While I reluctantly agreed to professional counseling, meeting with a third party did help to defuse a potentially heated situation. Hearing the details of his shenanigans, outlandish justifications for abruptly leaving the marriage, mixed with his declarations of love for his abandoned wife was infuriating and difficult to process. Although counseling did not result in a mended relationship, it helped me express my anger in a healthy way.

There are many ways to deal with anger in a healthy way. Some may choose to seek help from professional therapists and others may even attend anger management classes. To let go of anger you may also speak with close friends, exercise, shred paper (believe me, it helps), take up a sport that involves hitting a ball or heavy bag, meditate, read uplifting books, or do deep breathing exercises. As discussed in Chapter 1, journaling, can also help you manage and let go of your anger. Since there are a lot of things to be angry about after a breakup, write down all the things you are angry about and the people you are angry with. Even little things like eating dinner alone, watching TV, and doing repairs around the house can get you angry when you are reminded that you are now suddenly single without a partner to assist with chores. However, writing down all these little things in your journal can help to project this anger on paper instead of at other people. Whichever way you choose to express anger through healthy approaches, these suggestions will help you to release anger and lead to your own healing.

LETTING GO OF ANGER HELPS YOU MAKE TIMELY DECISIONS

Let's face it, an angry person has clouded thinking and cannot make rational or timely decisions during times of emotional crisis. The seriousness of timely decision-making may be emphasized by comparing the sudden shipwreck of the relationship to the disaster of a sinking ship. Stories have been told about it, books and movies have been written about it, and many people can recall one or more maritime errors that caused some of the world's greatest historical disasters at sea.

In most cases, the sinking of a vessel can be attributed to ignoring some sort of warning sign before, during, or while sailing that led to the tragedy. Some signs may be ominous like a change in temperature or weather, others may be cold and hostile like an iceberg, while some signs may be more subtle like the apathy of a captain omitting life-saving equipment he may have taken for granted. In some cases, boating disasters may happen without warning simply by accident even though all the safety precautions were followed.

Although the multiple loss of life during a disaster at sea cannot truly be compared in every aspect to the loss an individual suffers after the sudden end of a relationship, there are some comparisons worth reflecting upon. Similar to a maritime disaster, some may think that their relationship can overcome any obstacle, it can never suffer shipwreck, and if a disaster does happen, they may believe they are prepared to handle the unexpected damage on their own.

However, as evident in the comparative illustration, everyone needs tools and training to handle unforeseen events. In addition, you will also need help from others in one way or another to handle the emotional damage from a devastating breakup. It is unwise to attempt to go through a breakup alone. Therefore, timely recognizing warning signs, learning from others, controlling your emotional reactions, and developing the ability to quickly adapt to change may very well hold the key to your survival in times of emotional crisis.

RECOGNIZE THE SIGNS INDICATING THE RELATIONSHIP IS OVER

Did you miss your warning signs that the relationship was on its way to shipwreck? If you did miss the warning signs, be kind to yourself and know that you are not alone. Certainly, no one enters into a long-term relationship expecting that the union will face sudden shipwreck. However, while going through a sudden emotional crisis it is important to quickly adapt to change to avoid disaster as you navigate the fog of emotional suffering.

Although you may have been blindsided and have no contingency plan in place to cope with the sudden change in the relationship, it is crucial that you find a way to recognize warning signs that indicate the bond with your partner is truly unsalvageable. When someone you love tells you the relationship is over, believe them, even if those painful words were unexpected. There is no other warning sign clearer than someone speaking their truth from the heart. You may not agree with that truth, but it is their truth and you must accept it as such. Once you accept the truth that the relationship is over, you must then take action to adapt to the change thrown upon you.

It is a well-known reality that failed marriages outnumber those that succeed. Since most marriages may suffer shipwreck at some point, every failed relationship usually leaves behind broken lives, broken hearts, and wounded emotions in its path. Recognizing warning signs that the relationship is over and adapting to change are critical steps on the road to healing to protect your future. Could you not have seen the warning signs that led to the breakup? Many may have asked you this question about your failed relationship.

Sometimes it seems everyone will have an opinion about your breakup. From their perspective, some may assume there must have been bad behavior or changes from your ex that you should have seen months or even years in advance. Some may even accuse you of spoiling your ex with too much kindness, or enabling the end of your coupling by possibly hiding tension in the relationship to save face from public scrutiny. The judgment or indifference from others can go on and on. At times, this is the pressure society may place upon the surviving mate. The relentless gossip and opinions of folks with no first-hand knowledge of the situation can be just as insensitive as the abandonment itself. The reality is, in most if not all cases of sudden abandonment, when a person feels secure and protected in a long-term relationship, the warning signs only become visible when the relationship is already unilaterally shipwrecked.

This is the mystery with sudden breakups compared with divorce, which makes it hard to diagnose, get help, sympathy, or empathy to heal. People sometimes understand divorce because they see the warning signs leading up to separation or the divorce. Maybe they have seen public fights, tension in the relationship, infidelity, or some other indication there is discord in the relationship. However, in sudden breakups and abandonment cases, a person can be robbed of advance warning. As hard as it may seem for some to comprehend, in these cases the relationship can and does sometimes end without warning.

Reflections

Some warning signs that were not present in my marriage were: unhappiness, unexplained credit card charges or solo trips, past infidelity, changes in behavior or habits, arguments, or abusive treatments. In hindsight, I truly felt my relationship was on solid foundation until the day it abruptly ended. One warning sign that did show up in my relationship was financial incompatibility with regard to spending money. Whatever the reason behind the breakup, it is crucial that you find a way to recognize warning signs that indicate the bond with your partner is truly unsalvageable. When someone you love tells you the relationship is over, believe them, even if those painful words were unexpected. I had to take to heart my own advice and wasted no time beginning the healing process to bounce back after my breakup.

Some individuals who have been through a sudden

breakup or emotional abandonment may be able to recollect the times when they ignored one or more warning signs that their relationship was in trouble but not enough trouble to warrant the end of the relationship. If there were warning signs that you previously missed that certainly does not give anyone justification to hurt you by discarding you on such brutal terms.

So, if you've missed previous warning signs and now find yourself suddenly abandoned in a cold-blooded fashion, it is important that you stay calm to plan not just your survival but your magnificent rise to a new and improved you. Lashing out in anger or panicking about the "what ifs" will serve you no purpose whatsoever as you endeavor to find a resolution to the situation. It took a decision on your partner's part to end the relationship and it will take multiple decisions and rational thinking on your part to put the pieces of your life back together again.

HAVE A RATIONAL DISCUSSION

Master Your Emotions

The shock of not seeing the warning signs is usually followed by the emotional rollercoaster of anger. As discussed earlier, while anger is a natural reaction to the injustice you may have experienced, it must be kept in check since uncontrolled anger can make an already bad situation much worse. Therefore, to control anger, it is important to think before speaking, focus on the resolution to the conflict at hand instead of what caused the breakup, practice self-care, and know when to reach out for help to deal with the issue before you take reflex actions out of anger which you may later regret.

Anger is an impediment to your personal intelligence and acts as a hindrance to your mental clarity. Real solutions cannot be achieved with two angry people having heated exchanges during a breakup. Granted, staying calm and having a rational discussion with the person causing you pain is not the easiest feat to accomplish, especially when you are fighting for your own mental and emotional survival. However, staying calm and having a rational discussion allows you to:

1. Diffuse tension in the home;
2. Set boundaries and allow you to think clearly about the wisest and most peaceful ending for all the parties involved;
3. Regain the power that was taken away from you when you were discarded.

RATIONAL DISCUSSION HELPS DIFFUSE TENSION

How does having a rational discussion diffuse tension in the home? First, it helps you to maintain your inner peace and think clearly in situations that can affect your judgment and decision-making. If a person remains in a state of panic or anger it will not be possible to speak or act rationally. Panic, rage, and contentiousness cloud your judgment and make it virtually impossible to think of clear solutions to the problem you are faced with. Needless to say, panic and rational thinking are not friends. Certainly, remaining calm during turbulent periods in a relationship works wonders to diffuse tension in the home while you calmly hammer out plans to resolve the crisis you are confronted with.

While it is normal to feel personally hurt by the betrayal and hostility of your partner, it is equally important to remember that the bitterness from your partner may not even be personally directed at you. The guilty party may be so busy making plans to execute their own selfish decisions that hurting you personally may be the least of their worries. Reacting in an understanding manner and calmly controlling your emotions, attitude, and visual communication are critical actions you can take to de-escalate the tension within the dying relationship.

Having a rational discussion not only with your partner but with yourself will help you to control your emotions and focus on solutions. Even if you were suddenly abandoned without being afforded the opportunity to have a rational discussion, by controlling your emotions and redirecting your energies elsewhere, this intercepts the temptation to engage in unproductive behavior. If you are able to have a rational discussion with your partner after a breakup, be cordial and respectful so you can carefully mediate the transition from the life you knew to the one your partner forced you to accept.

RATIONAL DISCUSSION HELPS YOU SET BOUNDARIES

Secondly, having a rational discussion helps you adapt to new changes in the relationship and set boundaries on deciding how you both will manage communication going forward. Indeed, as hard as you may try, the relationship will never be the same after a sudden breakup. You may go from talking often to minimal communication or even no contact at all. When your partner announces his/her plans to discard you, calmly discuss the organized severing of assets, financial obligations, sharing responsibilities of children, if involved, and other matters of importance. Be clear about your boundaries, including those regarding sex, finances, personal memorabilia, and your time so there are no further complications or confusion.

By being objective and calmly engaging in sensible discussions, this type of concession will help you to think clearly about the wisest and most peaceful ending for all the parties involved. If you were denied the opportunity for further communication after being suddenly abandoned, think clearly of your next moves to find resources to help you restore peace, financial, and emotional stability in your home.

RATIONAL DISCUSSION WILL HELP YOU REGAIN YOUR POWER

Thirdly, expressing anger in healthy ways and having rational communication helps you regain your power. When your partner suddenly leaves the relationship without warning, they not only take your history and rob you of the future that you pictured spending a lifetime together, but they also shatter your identity, plunging you into emotional confusion. Losing your identity as a married person can undermine your values, faith, confidence, stability, and ability to trust. This sabotage of your character can be extremely traumatic and make you question the value of the life you shared with your partner and the sanctity of marriage or committed relationships in general.

Not only are you judged by family and friends, but society may label you as difficult, inexperienced, or incapable of keeping your partner grounded in a successful relationship. This change in status from being in a relationship to suddenly being single can take some serious mental adjustments and self-reflection. The swift ending of the relationship after a unilateral decision to go separate ways, in essence, cheats the other party from having the power to choose when and on what terms the relationship should end.

Having a rational discussion will help you learn to quickly adapt to the change in lifestyle from being in a relationship to suddenly living single. It will also help you to regain your power and identity that you may conclude was taken away from you when you were abandoned. You may not realize an important fact at the time you were discarded after a sudden breakup. You may have been stripped of the power to choose when the relationship ended but your power to choose what happens next in your life is something no one, not even your partner, can take away from you.

The power to turn your breakup into your greatest breakthrough is within you waiting to be accessed by you and you alone. Only you have the key to harness your power to make decisions under duress. Only you have the power to understand that you are not powerless but you just have not figured out how to tap into the energy that is already inside you. Begging, arguing, lashing out in anger, sobbing, or harping on why the relationship ended diminishes your power instead of strengthening it.

Similarly, worrying about what your partner is doing or who they will be dating is time wasted about a matter you have no control over. Both you and your partner have free will to choose and make individual decisions. Therefore, since you have no control over how your partner uses his or her free will, it is important to regain your power by speaking the truth to yourself, accepting that the relationship is over, and respecting the hasty decision of your partner to leave the relationship.

I know you may be going through a period of anguish that you may think is impossible to overcome, but rational thinking can help you find your inner self sooner rather than later. If you do take control of your tongue and thoughts, you will be able to clearly see through the emotional bewilderment and remember what you are really worth. Write down a list of positive and negative things about your partner, and do the same for yourself. Include everything you dislike about your partner from physical attributes to their acts of emotional treachery.

This list, labelled as a warning sign list, will help you keep a record of positive and negative character flaws not only in your partner but also in yourself. Instead of diminishing your character by being overly critical of yourself, give yourself credit for all your positive qualities and work on improving your negative characteristics to become better ones. Improving your inner self will redirect your time and energy towards yourself rather than getting angry about your failed relationship. A warning sign list with examples is on the next page. If you run out of space, you may continue this list on a separate piece of paper.

YOUR PARTNER'S WARNING SIGN LIST

CHARACTER

Negative		Positive
1.	Disloyal	Hard-working
2.	Indecisive	Intelligent
3.	Procrastinating	Easy going
4.		
5.		
6.		
7.		
8.		
9.		
10.		

YOUR WARNING SIGN LIST

CHARACTER

	Negative	Positive
1.	Impatient	Loyal
2.	Strong-willed	Determined
3.	Stubborn	Innovative
4.		
5.		
6.		
7.		
8.		
9.		
10.		

So how long is your warning sign list and what did it reveal about you and your ex? Did your list help you make your own decision whether you will or will not take your partner back into your life after you've been brutally discarded? The reality is, if you would not give the keys to your home to a stranger to come and go as they please, why would you give your partner who betrayed you the keys to your heart to enter and exit whenever he or she pleases? Would you not set boundaries for your partner as you would this stranger? Would you not do a risk assessment to determine if you could withstand any losses if you take your partner back and possibly be discarded again?

Did your personal warning sign list reveal you are living against your authentic self? Did it reveal you are living against your own truth? Did your list remind you of how valuable you already are? Whatever revelations you discovered after coming up with your warning sign list, this exercise will not make the next decisions in your relationship for you, but it will help you deal with the realities of the next step, overcoming denial.

Four reminders to help you let go of anger:

1. Recognize anger is a normal reaction to your breakup but acting on the anger is not appropriate.
2. Find healthy ways to let go of unhealthy anger by seeking help from others, exercise, and self-care.
3. Recognize and accept the warning signs that the relationship is really over.
4. Letting go of anger will help you have rational discussions and give you the clarity needed for critical decision-making. Rational discussions will help you diffuse tension, set boundaries, and regain your power.

JOURNAL COMMENTARY

What angered me most about my breakup was

____

____

The phrases that resonated with me in this chapter

____

____

I find it difficult to let go of anger because

____

____

After reading this chapter I realize

____

____

I accept the truth that I

____

____

Today I am not the victim but the victor because

____

____

When you feel like you have become the champion over your experience, when you feel like you have become your own warrior, immediately discard this page. Safely burn it and watch the page disintegrate into ashes. Whatever you do, after you feel emotionally complete, just let it go.

CHAPTER 3

OVERCOMING DENIAL

Choose Healing Over Pain

Delays and denials are embargos to your transformation.

GROWING UP, ONE OF MY fondest memories was going to my uncle's beach house almost every summer in the Caribbean. It was not a fancy place but a small cabin he built beachside on a tiny island off the coast in the Republic of Trinidad and Tobago called Saut d'Eau. The waters surrounding the cabin were clear like glass and resurrected the feelings of the serenity I enjoyed at my Granny's house.

One summer morning, I had one of the most frightening experiences of my life. We were heading home after spending weeks at the beach. Although we knew there was an afternoon flash storm approaching, we delayed our departure from the beach earlier that morning. My uncle was an experienced fisherman but was a blasé kind of man who remained unruffled by my grandmother's persistence to get him to expedite our departure. As he took his cool time packing the boat, I was beginning to wonder why my grandmother was dramatizing events as the sea waters were calm and there were clear blue skies as far as the eyes could see.

As we departed the beach in this tiny fishing boat and reached in the middle of the ocean, mid-point to our destination, the weather took a dramatic and unexpected turn. The blue skies suddenly turned gray, giving way to rain as the calm seas we left behind quickly turned violent. Without warning we were riding giant waves that dwarfed our tiny fishing boat. My uncle was a risk-taker, but he knew we were in serious danger and there was no room for error. The waves were so turbulent that my uncle had to strap his leg onto the boat and his arm on the shift lever that controlled the motor. None of the passengers in the boat except my uncle knew how to swim in deep waters and none of us were wearing life jackets.

Riding waves that were thirty to fifty feet high was bumpy and blistering; there was no pit stop or dry land in sight. The journey through those rough seas was frightening to say the least. As the giant waves rapidly approached us splashing against the boat, we held on to every part of that wooden vessel for dear life as the boat went air borne over every wave it conquered. At the time, I was certain one of my fondest childhood memories was going to be written down in history as a deadly tragedy.

Thankfully, to the contrary, we made it to dry land alive, bruised, and drenched with sea water. It was a combination of navigational skills by an experienced fisherman and a divine miracle we made it to shore safely. The ocean won my respect, but the reality of this experience was that delay and denial of a potential storm nearly cost us our lives that day. As discussed in Chapter 2, panic and rational thinking are not friends. Likewise, denial and delay are traitors and enemies of facts and logic. Denial was almost catastrophic for me during this personal maritime experience and so too denial can be disastrous during the stages of healing from emotional abandonment wounds after a breakup.

While denial is a natural coping mechanism of the brain to deal with sudden trauma, studies have shown that staying in a state of denial beyond a reasonable time can cause real injury to the brain. If you are at this juncture in your emotional journey, and you postpone getting help to heal, you are really in danger of entering into an abysmal downward spiral into depression.

Reflections

I felt those emotional injuries when I went through my cycle of denial after my breakup. I felt great fear for my future, stress about financial worries, and panic over loneliness when I thought about who would be there for me to lean on if I started drowning under the weight of life's daily burdens. These emotions lingered in my head as if I was in a never-ending labyrinth of danger and planted me in a state of constant fight or flight.

Since the brain is associated with a person's memory and emotional responses, it can really be affected by traumatic stress if left unchecked. Therefore, as you go through the various stages of emotional grief after your breakup, you must find resources to quickly maneuver out of the brink of depression without delay to avoid any lasting negative effects on your mind, body, and soul. For the brain to process solutions to your problems it has to come out of this state of shock and denial during the grief process, before it can finally accept the need to overcome these emotional reactions. The good news is, while the brain can be negatively impacted by emotional trauma, there is also evidence to support the fact that the brain can be healed over time.

The brain is truly a magnificent organ that is capable of great self-healing. There are millions of success stories from warriors who have conquered adversities in life that could teach you the great power you possess in recognizing the brain's ability to heal itself. As much as you may be in emotional pain at the moment, your brain is actively working to mobilize damage control mechanisms to make you have great experiences again. All you have to do is give your mind the tools and new memories it needs to repair the emotional damage you sustained after your breakup.

As a society we are still learning about the full capabilities of the brain but most of us know that the brain is made up of an organized circuit that controls the body. It transmits not only information but also stores and rewrites memories. Some memories are good, some bad, and some memories like names, places, colors, and odors are all stored as information in our brain. If you do stay in a state of denial indefinitely, you may actually be robbing your brain's ability to take action to store good memories so you can heal from this stage of grief.

Notice how open and honest children are about the things they're afraid of such as: insects, monsters, water, and darkness. But as they grow into adulthood learning new experiences, the brain over time will learn to build new memories to overwrite old memories of things they were once afraid of. As an adult, to overcome denial after a breakup you must similarly be open to allowing your brain to experience new things that will help you heal from denial by:

- Being honest about your fears and insecurities.
- Expressing those fears and emotions by speaking to a trusted person and journaling about the experience.
- Having the courage to face the fact that there is a problem that requires a resolution.
- Taking action to avoid negative consequences by seeking professional help or joining a support group.

You can become resilient as you seek to overcome the negative emotions after your breakup. The brain can change its circuitry and emotional responses about your breakup experience and adapt by learning new things to create new memories and skills. Since you are designed and capable of adapting to change, work without delay to rebuild a healthy mind if you are deeply affected by the emotional effects of abandonment.

To rebuild the mind and damaged emotions after a traumatic breakup, it is important that you don't stay too long in the denial stage. Why? Because living indefinitely in the denial stage makes accepting facts and the realities about your life much harder. Denial also makes achieving progress towards healing and personal success almost impossible. There are two choices to make during the denial stage. The path to PAIN or to HEALING.

PAIN OR HEALING

What Will You Choose?

P (PAIN) - You are shocked at hearing the initial news that you are being discarded. The shock is so severe it blocks your ability to get angry and your body goes into a fight or flight state. At this initial stage you feel like your emotional foundation was shattered and pulled like a rug from under your feet without warning. You are vulnerable and feel stunned from the trauma of what it feels like to survive the impact of the train wreck your relationship was reduced to. The sadness is overwhelming as the theft of your identity as a partnered person is shattered and all the memories you shared are suddenly washed away in a flash flood. Your future seems uncertain as you are catapulted from a solid foundation and plunged into a real emotional crisis.

Conflicted with unfinished sentences, words, and what if's that were left unsaid, you are left feeling incomplete and you are left to pick up the pieces of the broken relationship. The devastation over the sudden loss of what you thought was a healthy relationship results in real pain; so much so you would do almost anything to stop the pain. The pain causes some to beg, plead, act irrationally, or try to salvage the one-sided relationship because of shared history, kids, financial comfort, or just to save face from the label or judgment from society.

A (ANGER) - As you travel down the dark road of pain and self-pity these emotions intersect with anger. Your life feels like it is under attack, and your rage is swift. You resent your ex for throwing your life into disarray. For this disturbance of your peace, you want to play the role of executioner to dismantle any new accomplishments of your former companion in the same way your life was dismantled. The need to pass on your pain to the one who caused you pain is strong. The need for revenge, restitution, impeachment, and passing on blame is the only way you feel justified in suffering such devastating emotional pain and loss. This stage of anger, if uncontrolled and left unchecked, is destructive to yourself and others.

I (ISOLATION) - The desire to survive the stage of anger causes you to be at war with yourself and internalize the emotional abuse you suffered. After being abandoned and denied the opportunity to unleash your anger to the fullest extent on your former companion, you begin to suffer withdrawal symptoms. You are insecure and feel like you have failed while carrying out one of the most important tasks of your life, a committed relationship. You feel like your body was ejected from your life without your permission and you resent watching life moving on without you while you are left behind wounded like roadkill on a highway with no one stopping to bandage you up.

You blame yourself for not seeing the danger sooner or how you contributed to the breakup altogether. Your anxiety is intense and trust in people becomes distorted as you replay the scene of the breakup over and over in your head until it becomes branded in your memory. You begin to lose sleep and maybe your health. You feel there is no way out of the cycle of anger, pain, and loneliness, which eventually leads to depression if you delay in finding a way out. Trapped in your own criticism and self-blame, the isolation and loneliness are indescribable and the emptiness is deafening.

N (NEEDY) - Self-blame causes you to feel unworthy of love, needy, desperate for a return to normalcy. You feel like you have lost control of your life and the damage to your self-esteem feeds off you like a leech deep inside your core system. Any glimmer of sunlight seems to get overshadowed by wounds of abandonment thrown over you like a blanket, draining what's left of your energy. The emotional stockpile which was restrained by anger and isolation opens up and you are extremely vulnerable.

This state of need is where self-sabotage is most likely to be at its pinnacle, leading to self-defeating patterns of self-dereliction. It is the stage where most people make the mistake of entering into another relationship prematurely without first healing. It is the time when you can enter self-destructive rebound relationships to redeem what you think is your lost self-esteem. It is this stage of need where that cycle of abandonment along with emotional abuse can reoccur again and again. You are at a crossroads and faced with the choice to return to the broken relationship or carry the dead weight and unhealthy behaviors into a new half-baked relationship.

Pain is inescapable. It is an inevitable part of life and unavoidable in the aftermath of broken relationships. Though pain may be unavoidable, it can produce positive characteristics like strength, courage, endurance, determination, growth, and a better you, but only if you continue to take action, make the right choices, and never lose hope. Hope is the alternative choice you have over a life of pain.

THE POWER OF HOPE

The Path to Healing

H (HOPE) - Lack of hope feeds the fears behind abandonment. However, hope gives you power and makes the present burden of emotional pain and hardship easier to bear. Therefore, you should never allow yourself to drown in disappointment while losing the lifeline of boundless hope. If you lose all hope, you will lose your battle to live a better life. Learn from the past, believe that things will get better, and work hard to counteract negative painful traits. Every storm has an ending no matter how devastating and you are never alone while going through your storm. There is always someone whose experiences you can draw strength from.

Take responsibility for your actions and avoid blaming others for your pain. If you keep blaming others for your emotional pain, you will not take responsibility to fix your own pain. Your life is actually your responsibility to repair and maintain, so if something is broken in your life you must take the steps to fix it. Hope is the belief that vanquishes entrenched feelings of self-pity, isolation, desperation, and can rekindle positive emotions to propel you forward. Hope can ignite imagination, strength, and courage you didn't think were possible to possess. Hope is the music that soothes you in those moments of loneliness on the road to healing. It is the tonic for your pain and the compass that will guide you in your darkest hour.

E (ENERGIZE) - With hope burning bright you are wounded but energized to fight for your life and rewire your brain to become successful. Hope fuels your drive and gives you power to transform bad experiences into opportunities for tremendous growth. Through hope your brain is empowered to reach its fullest potential and use your precious time to replace negative thinking with ideas, dreams, and goals worthy of your attention. Be proud of yourself and be patient with the journey.

Stay away from people who are not aligned with your goals or who can trigger you into negative thinking that can sabotage the building of a stronger self. Set short-term and long-term goals for self-improvement and go after those goals with a vengeance. Feed your mind by reading, meditating, and speaking with those who have triumphed over their own trials. Focus on tomorrow's triumphs and don't wallow over yesterday's defeats.

A (ACCEPTANCE) - Accept the relationship is over or would not be the same after the breakup. To live in denial that you were abandoned will not change these facts. Acceptance is part of the process to forgive and the antidote for resentment. It is the path forward, not simply to forget the major emotional changes you've been through or to understand all the "whys," but to get a clearer vision of how to achieve success in your new life.

Acceptance is taking responsibility for what went wrong in your relationship even though it was not your fault you were emotionally hurt and abandoned. Acceptance breathes contentment and understanding about your grief during the healing process after your breakup. It is recognizing that you cannot change the details of your breakup, but it is a turning point in your mind that you are willing to change your own negative thoughts and behaviors.

L (LOVE) - Love yourself, invest in yourself, lift yourself out of pain, swim with the tide not against it, and liberate yourself from the bondage of self-blame. Repurpose your life by making healthy lifestyle changes, getting rest, and creating goals. Reward yourself at each stage you accomplish healing. Keep a journal, do creative activities that force your brain to become distracted with positive things. Give yourself an outlet to express emotions through creativity. Pick up a hobby, listen to positive music, and get involved with activities that make you happy. Talk to someone trustworthy who will just listen when thoughts seem overwhelming. Loving yourself and learning to still love and trust others will help you understand that a person does not lose love after abandonment, but they retain their reservoir of love to share with those who demonstrate that they are worthy of it.

From these stages of pain to healing, if you do meditate and overcome the denial stage in your emotional journey, you will realize the choice is yours to live a life of pain or one of hope and healing. As bleak as your trauma may seem at the moment, if you persist on the road to healing, there will always be a breakthrough. No storm will last forever; it must end, and your storm will end too, if you choose to heal.

Four reminders to help you overcome denial:

1. To avoid depression, don't postpone getting help to heal from the stage of denial.
2. Delays and denials are embargos to your transformation.
3. Our magnificent brain can learn to rewrite negative experiences and replace these with positive ones. But you must take action.
4. Choose hope instead of pain and accept responsibility for your own healing.

JOURNAL COMMENTARY

The most painful part about my breakup was

____

____

The phrases that resonated with me in this chapter

____

____

I find it difficult to let go of denial because

____

____

After reading this chapter I realize hope is important because

____

____

I accept the truth that I

____

____

Today I am not the victim but the victor because

____

____

When you feel like you have become the champion over your experience, when you feel like you have become your own warrior, immediately discard this page. Put the page through a shredder. Whatever you do, after you feel emotionally complete, just let it go.

CHAPTER 4

HEALING FROM BLAME

Coping With Spiritual & Emotional Loss

Blaming someone else is easy but it solves nothing. It only rearranges your problems to be the same.

THERE ISN'T ONE WORD THAT could aptly describe the devastation a person feels after being abandoned from a sudden breakup. You're probably still trying to make sense of all your emotions tangled together in wounds you are still working hard to heal. Maybe you feel like a failure, a loser, or feel like the entire breakup was your fault. Your life was turned upside down and you are still struggling to find stability again. Remember, you are not alone. Many people are making every effort at this very moment to combat self-blame and the overwhelming feeling of failure. Blaming yourself and others for what did or didn't happen solves nothing. It just keeps your brain in that negative loop of thinking on a road going nowhere in search of a solution.

The reality is, breakups and divorce have become commonplace within society and across all cultures. You've read my breakup story, but you've probably also read stories of other individuals who were left through all sorts of ridiculous, cowardly methods. Some were left while pregnant, by phone, by email, via a third party, social media, text messages. Others did not even get the courtesy of a verbal conversation before realizing they were suddenly abandoned and the relationship was over. For some individuals, being robbed of the opportunity to have a decent dialogue as to why the relationship ended so suddenly is the part that is especially devastating and more painful than the sudden abandonment itself. To be loved unconditionally one day then abandoned the next day without explanation is as heartless as it could get for anyone going through a breakup.

Despite all the tragic stories of how you were left by your ex and the sordid details of your breakup, it is important not to carry the burden of blame and shame on your shoulders. Sure, you've experienced what you may feel as a fall from grace, but don't get caught up in the cycle of internalizing what society may label as failure. Your breakup does not mean you are a failure, it just means you are in one of the stages of your transformation. As discussed in the previous chapters, the emotional pain from a breakup is inescapable but it is survivable.

The impetus to blame is sometimes a natural reaction to deflect the pain caused when someone hurt you. While blaming others may seem like the easy route to take when faced with a problem, It is a deflection from honesty, courage, and the action you must take for true healing. Blame is what it is. It is the boldface lie we tell ourselves while acting as if mistakes were not part of our human experience. Sometimes you may blame others to project your pain, anger, mistakes, hardships, and other conflicts away from you to the person in the path where your finger is pointing. But the more you blame others, the more you will reinforce the toxic pattern of lies that the breakup was all a big pile of failure and it's your entire fault or your ex's fault or somebody's fault. The courage and work involved in facing negative experiences and taking responsibility for your healing is the challenging route you will have to take to really be successful.

SPIRITUAL LOSS

Mistakes are part of the human existence. From the time we connected with our mother in the womb and at birth we begin learning to trust. Since we don't live in a perfect world, over time that trust we develop as children gets challenged again and again. The people we love may make mistakes or deliberately commit acts to hurt us. Throughout a lifetime, individuals can store generational abandonment wounds recording various ruptures in their ability to trust that can imprint their minds. This mental imprint can occur if you grew up with absentee parents, a divorce in the family, experienced physical or emotional abuse as a child, rejection, death of someone you loved, or some other memorable trauma.

Nonetheless, through the ups and downs of childhood and disappointments in life, most people are generally taught that there is still a "happily ever after" where you can feel safe and unguarded. That place where you eventually feel protected, happy, and vulnerable is with your family, spiritual advisors, spouse, and friends within your close community. In this supportive environment, over time you learn to love and maintain trust.

However, after dropping your guard and learning to trust once again as an adult by getting involved in a committed consensual relationship, it can be devastating when your partner suddenly abandons you. This break in trust by your partner can trigger the breaches of trust you experienced as a child. This trial can betray a person's entire belief system regarding the permanence of marriage. After abandonment, your foundation shifts, your spiritual equilibrium is disrupted, and your entire network of friends is turned upside down.

Suddenly, the abandoned individual is also misunderstood or shunned by mutual family and friends who underestimated the complexity of the damage done to the surviving partner after the breakup. People you were once close to as a couple may suddenly distance their contact with you since they may not know what to say or feel able to deal with the awkwardness of the fallout from your breakup. Double dates, movie nights, and associations with mutual acquaintances can swiftly turn into painful memories, even for those who used to be in your inner circle of friends. Society often brands a failed relationship as the guilt between two parties who grew apart without realizing how different abandonment cases are to those of mutual breakups.

Often times, people are unable to acknowledge even the possibility that the marriage could have ended due to the guilt of one party. I've heard some say, "It takes two to break up a relationship," "You spoiled him, that's why he left," "You must have done something wrong," "There are three sides to a story," or "Well, you know you are career-driven so maybe you were not present enough in the relationship." That list of speculations and misconceptions from people with their own opinions is never-ending.

In sudden abandonment cases everyone, including spiritual advisors, seems to have their own philosophies about the reasons for the broken relationship, but only those who have been through relationship abandonment can accurately explain the intricacies about the experience. It is this lack of understanding about the complexities of abandonment after a breakup that appears to be one of the reasons spiritual and emotional support systems for abandoned spouses are minimal and inadequate at best.

Communities and cultures are no more forgiving while looking at the sudden breakup under their own lenses. Branded by society as a deadbeat who could not hold on to the affection of their partner, in shame we may walk around shackled by what we think others will think of us or what is taboo in our modern society. We inappropriately assume shame for disappointing others who may be sarcastically thinking, *"The once happy couple may not be invincible after all,"* or those who rationalize, *"If the perfect marriage can crumble then there is no hope for lesser mortals."*

These self-defeating thoughts are the very lines of thinking that can obscure your recognition that the failed relationship was not your fault, just like the breaches of trust you've experienced throughout your childhood were not your fault. Without seeing the selfish decisions of your spouse for what they are, some may go crawling back to a lifeless relationship because it feels safe, to pacify ingrained teaching about subjection, or to satisfy the wishes of friends and family.

It is easy to resort to blaming everyone, including

yourself. However, not only do you have to put shame and blame in its place, you also must unburden from your shoulders the guilt you feel after surviving the failed relationship. If married you may feel guilty for failing God, failing the institution of marriage and the serious vows you took, and failing society's status that comes with being a married couple. You may feel guilt for failing your family, guilt from the loss of friends and the change in relationships due to your new single status. You probably feel guilty that you have failed yourself.

The one thing you thought you could have done right, the one thing you thought could have halted the generational curse of dysfunction you may have been raised from, you fumbled. Your hands tremble when you fill out those forms that ask for your marital status. You're no longer married, separated, divorced, or single, but just in emotional limbo. The pen hovers over the married box and you reluctantly circle single hoping you won't be judged by the person reviewing the form. These small things like filling out a form are reminders that your status has changed, and you blame your partner for suddenly placing you in this quandary.

Apart from the blame you may attribute to your former partner and guilt from the perception of society, you must also deal with your own self-criticism and self-condemnation. Self-blame is the personal browbeating you give yourself when the relationship comes undone. Even if it's not your fault you annoy yourself to death that you may have somehow contributed to the collapse of the relationship. Women especially do this to themselves.

You may feel like your critics may be right, maybe you did spoil him, nagged him, changed him, physically changed your own mind, gained weight, lost weight, or didn't do enough to be appealing to him. You may blame yourself for not seeing the warning signs in time so you could've done better. You may blame yourself for jeopardizing or misplacing your trust and you may blame yourself for blindly entrusting your partner with the fragile parts of your heart.

The stain on his shirt, the missed phone call from the other woman, the time he came home late with an explanation that didn't make sense, and all the small instances you brushed aside as insignificant now begin to make sense and come together like pieces of a puzzle you created in your head. But as you play these scenes to piece together how and why the relationship failed, now you blame yourself for not acting to protect yourself. But as the above quote highlights, blame solves nothing. It only rearranges the same problem to be the same problem. Blaming solves nothing but taking responsibility for your healing resolves everything.

HOW TO OVERCOME THE CYCLE OF BLAME

While it is important to rebuild your spirituality and your ability to trust, it is equally important to remember that shame, guilt, and self-blame love the dark places where we hide our secrets but vanish when we bring them to the light. Speaking to others you trust about your spiritual and emotional abandonment after the trauma of a breakup can go a long way to help you on this journey to heal. In essence, speaking about your bad experiences takes away the power of shame, guilt, and self-blame. Remember, overcoming the emotional and spiritual loss of abandonment is not your shame or guilt to bear but your truth to accept. The more you take responsibility for what happens in your life and speak the truth about it, the greater your chances of healing from the tendency of casting blame on others.

Another way to overcome blame is to practice self-awareness. Work on getting to the point where you catch yourself mid-sentence when you are in the process of blaming others. Maybe your ex blamed you for everything that happened before and after the breakup. Maybe you feel the need to reciprocate the blame and point fingers at your ex for blaming you. Stop listening to and stop playing the broken song in your head compelling you to continue the cycle of blame. If you peel away the layers of blame, you may very well find the truth beneath your intentions. And the truth is, you may be blaming others to escape doing the work to heal your own insecurities, expectations, fears, and vulnerabilities. As you become self-aware you will gain more understanding of yourself to help you resist the impulse to unduly blame others and yourself.

A third way to overcome blame is to keep nurturing positive thinking. Take a look at your warning sign list in Chapter 2 and ponder over all the positive qualities you listed about yourself. Warriors go through training to develop the right mental fitness to face many challenges. Similarly, to overcome blame you must also work hard to replace negative thinking with positive thoughts and understanding. Remind yourself how successful you already are and celebrate the strides you are making each day to become a better person. Each progress you make towards healing, you will realize that grief and growth can coexist if you stay in motion and resist the temptation to blame others. Keep feeding your mind with positive thoughts and soon you will realize you've become a mighty warrior, ready for the next challenge to build a new life again.

Four reminders to help you overcome blame:

1. Your breakup does not mean you are a failure, it just means you are in the stages of your own transformation.
2. Blaming others and self-blame solves nothing.
3. Blame is the boldface lie we tell ourselves while acting as if mistakes were not part of our human experience.
4. Pain from emotional and spiritual loss is inevitable after a breakup but it is survivable. Speaking with others about your pain, self-awareness, and positive thinking will diffuse pain and help you overcome the impulse to blame.

JOURNAL COMMENTARY

I blame my ex for everything because

____

____

I find it difficult to trust when

____

____

The phrases that resonated with me in this chapter

____

____

I find it difficult to stop blaming others because

____

____

Today I realize I am ready to

____

____

Today I am not the victim but the victor because

____

____

When you feel like you have become the champion over your experience, when you feel like you have become your own warrior, immediately discard this page. Give the page to your pets so they can have a field day with it. Whatever you do, after you feel emotionally complete, just let it go.

These journal commentaries to yourself about your relationship may seem trivial but they are powerful. You have advanced your authority over your own emotions and released the energy of the emotional weights chipping away at your progress. Now you are ready to take on the next step in your journey, to conquer your financial loss.

CHAPTER 5

COPING WITH FINANCIAL LOSS

Lessons from lions and life—courage is not for the spineless.

WE CERTAINLY CANNOT GET THROUGH discussing a traumatic breakup without addressing the financial impact it will have on both parties and the road to recovery from financial loss. Inevitably, a discussion about money will have to be addressed. Whatever unpaid debt you have together will now have to be dissected. The change in your financial status may hurt a bit if your ex used to pay half the monthly bills.

You may have to say no to a lot of spending habits you were once used to. Sometimes you will have to say no to family members, no to in-laws, no to friends, or no to your employer. By far the hardest no you may have to utter is to your ex. It takes courage to say no to your heart, especially when it comes to the person you love. While it is essential to stop the bleeding of your figurative heart, it is also important to make sure you don't bleed out financially.

Think about it. If a bank loaned you money for a mortgage but you defaulted on the loan or filed for bankruptcy, what would be your chances of getting an immediate second chance for a loan with the same bank without a proper explanation and plan of action to right the wrongs of your financial shortcomings? While money cannot be evaluated on the same scale as people, the rationale certainly explains why you will have to decide if you would lend your love again to someone who previously squandered it or cut your losses and invest your emotions with someone more responsible and deserving. Banks are in the lending business but so are you every time you extend your love, your time, and yourself to a person.

Reflections

I learned that love is not bulletproof. When you hurt a person and the damage done to that person becomes irretrievable, that love may not be available to you if and when you return to beg for it. Therefore, in my case, when my husband returned to ask back for the love he once had from me, I didn't really have it readily available to give back to him at the time, especially without proper reassurance that my love would not be misused again in the future. The courage you need to make tough decisions to protect your heart is the similar courage you will need to protect your finances.

Making the decision to fix your marriage or let it go is a life-altering choice only you can make. It is, therefore, a decision that cannot be taken lightly. Even though the damage done to your failed relationship may not be your fault, the reality is, you are the one responsible for stopping the emotional and financial hemorrhage. You are the one responsible for deciding what is best for you going in or coming out of the breakup.

"I DO . . ."

Those words, "I do," and "till death do us part," mean something to each couple who decide to walk down the aisle and begin a new life together towards the same destination, the "happily ever after." Unless there is malicious intent from the very beginning of the relationship, no one goes into a marriage thinking it will soon be over. The reality is one of the most overlooked aspects of being abandoned after a breakup is dealing with the financial damage that could be inflicted on the surviving spouse in the aftermath of the failed relationship. More often than not, some individuals who relinquished all financial control to their marriage mate and stay in the dark about finances during the relationship will find it harder to make monetary adjustments when they suddenly find themselves solo after the sudden breakup.

Therefore, while married and in a healthy relationship, it is better to share financial responsibilities, or at least be acquainted with enough information about the household's finances. In this way, you will be better positioned to make settlements that will help you maintain the same standard of living after the relationship is over. The unavoidable reality after becoming companionless is that you will be the captain of your own ship whether you are ready or not. You will be responsible for your own financial future which will include savings, expenses, and investments after the failed relationship.

Let's face the facts, bills will keep coming whether you break up or not, and the banks, landlords, and all the other creditors will expect timely payments without really any concern about your financial loss. So you should expect creditors may sympathize with you about your emotional and financial loss but they will ask for payment all in the same sentence. Actually, after your breakup, it may seem as if the same bills from creditors will show up in the mailbox twice a month! There is no way to sugarcoat these realities. If you are not independently wealthy, you will have serious financial responsibilities and decisions to make to reduce your living expenses so you can manage your lifestyle on a reduced household income.

If you find yourself facing financial trouble after this reduced income, don't ask "Why me?" or get frustrated and anxious. Remember, it takes courage to face the realities of your finances and this quality is certainly not for the spineless. These adversities are really not your enemy but they are your friends, holding a mirror to your life to teach you who you really are and who you can become. There will be plenty of time to grieve, whine, and eat tubs of ice cream over the breakup. More importantly, for your own financial survival, it is critical that you assess your household and net worth as soon as possible to control the financial impact of shifting, in most cases, from a higher to lower income household.

FOUR STEPS TO TIE A FINANCIAL TOURNIQUET

Four steps to managing the impact of financial loss after a breakup are:

1. Gather and organize all your financial records.

   Such records include real estate title, property deed(s), income and/or business tax returns, stocks, bank statements, credit card statements, retirement accounts, and all other brick and mortar financial documents.

   Basically, all the documents that help assess your financial standing. The sooner you can take a snapshot of your financial status to assess your assets and expenses, the better.

   Remember your expenses may not have increased but your overall household income more than likely will have decreased. Create a spreadsheet listing all your household monthly income and expenses. If this task seems overwhelming, employ the assistance of your tax preparer or accountant.

   Income includes: Salaries and wages, bonuses

and tips, child support, pensions, social security, dividends, royalties, and all other miscellaneous income.

Expenses will include: Mortgage payments, car note payments, real estate, medical and car insurances, life insurance, credit card, childcare, school tuition, food, travel expenses, child care costs, entertainment, and all other miscellaneous household expenses.

Since the cost for medical and disability insurance coverage can change year after year, it will be necessary to reevaluate these costs occasionally to determine if you will need to purchase new health insurance. Some home insurance premiums automatically increase annually, so it is important for you to review these policies to ensure you will not be paying extra money for coverage you do not need.

Usually it is appropriate to review all your insurance policies annually to make sure you have enough coverage or reduce the premiums if necessary. Be sure to remove your ex as beneficiary from all investment accounts and medical insurance policies.

Make a list of all your investments such as: real estate, businesses, stocks, bonds, IRAs, liquid cash, and any other monetary savings.

After gathering all these documents, calculate your net worth to assess how much money you have on hand to begin your solo financial life. Your net worth is calculated by subtracting your total liabilities (what you owe) from your total assets (what you own), to give you an overall snapshot of your financial standing. There are plenty of net worth calculators and worksheets online to help you assess your financial standing.

If you are in the negative financial status don't let this scare you into immobility. After a breakup many people may not have enough money in the bank to barely support one month of expenses. Not the best financial position to be in or stay in. Sometimes the financial impact of a breakup may mean you will not be able to afford any extended sick absences from work, take another vacation, eat out at restaurants, or buy new clothes. For others, a breakup may mean you will have to depend on government subsidies or social services until you regain your financial footing again. If you are going through a breakup that negatively impacted your bank account, know that you can put your financial life back together again and rise from the ashes to live the comfortable lifestyle you had before your financial life became disrupted.

2. Close joint bank and credit card accounts.

   Establish individual banking, savings, and investment accounts if you don't already have these in place. One of the most important accounts you can set up is an emergency savings account. This type of buffer account will prepare you for any unexpected events and help you weather the expenses of sudden job loss, medical emergencies, household repairs, and other financial curve balls life may throw at you. Strive to save enough to get to an emergency fund equal to about six months to one year of annual income.

   Negotiate with creditors for lower interest or monthly payments now that your household income has changed. Many creditors are willing to negotiate better lending terms or interest rates when you approach them with a reasonable and workable plan to continue monthly payments. Take necessary steps to find out your credit score and work to improve this score immediately. Equifax, Experian, and TransUnion are the three credit bureaus that independently track data from your credit history. While you are entitled to a free annual credit report from AnnualCreditReport.com, most lenders who manage your individual checking and saving accounts also have products to help you check your credit score status.

To improve your credit score it is important that you:

- Pay your bills on time.
- Reduce your overall credit card balances.
- Don't exceed any of your credit card limits.
- Establishing long-term credit trade line history.
- Report any inaccuracies found on your credit to the credit bureaus.

Any inaccuracies on your credit can be challenged by writing to the credit bureaus, putting a fraud alert on your credit report, and frequently monitoring your credit activities.

3. Create a budget.

After steps 1 and 2 are completed, it will be much easier to create a budget. Creating a budget will help you identify which set of expenses can be eliminated and areas you may need to downsize. For me, I eliminated cable and the telephone landline monthly bills since I was very rarely at home. Sometimes I felt like a stranger in my own home, only showing up to sleep after long days at work and college. While those small adjustments worked for me, you must evaluate your life to implement lifestyle changes that will help you live within your means.

These lifestyle changes may include moving into a smaller living space, cutting back on cable or streaming service subscriptions, reducing cell phone costs or miscellaneous spending like dining out, gym memberships, or the weekly trip to the manicurist and hair salon. If cash is tight, you may have to explore ways to earn extra income from a second job or exploring your own talents to start a side hustle.

Whatever changes you make to stick to your budget be sure to restrict panic buying and avoid the temptation of taking on new credit card debt. These changes do not have to be permanent but can certainly help you maintain financial buoyancy to weather any initial monetary crisis.

4. Save.

Save, save, and save. Immediately start automating your finances by setting up processes that put money into your savings account as soon as you receive income payments. After receiving your income and allocating funds for savings, pay your bills as soon as you received them. The money left over after this automatic process of paying yourself first then paying creditors can then be used for everyday lifestyle spending. Part of developing a saving mentality includes buying groceries in bulk or at discounted prices, packing lunch to take to work, and canceling subscriptions you no longer use.

These four steps were of great help to me and certainly protected me against any short-term or long-term financial calamity. If you are going through the experience of a sudden breakup don't delay to seek out positive advice from others to help you on your journey towards self-improvement and financial success. Instead of worrying about your current financial situation, feed your mind on wholesome thoughts that will drive you to success instead of financial stagnation. Read books that will help sharpen your financial decision-making.

There are plenty of stories of people who have beaten the odds and traversed against impossible obstacles to become successful. What separates those who succeed from those who fail are, among other things, courage, determination, perseverance, taking action, and feeding positive thoughts into your mind. Join alliances with positive advisors and find your list of books that will heighten your financial awareness so you will be mobilized to make advancements towards achieving financial success. This will be the most courageous step you can take to ensure you don't suffer any permanent financial harm or long-term setbacks with money after your breakup.

Four reminders to help you cope with financial loss:

1. Make a final decision if you will recycle the relationship or call it quits for good.
2. Learn to say no to nonessentials. Tie an emotional and financial tourniquet so you don't bleed out.
3. Follow the four steps to tie a financial tourniquet by:

    i. Organizing all financial records.
    ii. Closing joint bank and credit card accounts. Establish new individual accounts.
    iii. Create a budget and stick to it.
    iv. Save like your life depends on it, because it does.

4. Read investment books and align yourself with financial professionals who can help you get back on track with your money management goals and other financial affairs.

JOURNAL COMMENTARY

Today my net worth is

The phrases that resonated with me in this chapter

I realize I need help to

Today I created a budget for

Today I made a financial goal to

CHAPTER 6

PRACTICE THE ART OF GRATITUDE

Gratitude is taking note of the little things while learning to forgive big things.

AFTER ACCEPTING FINANCIAL REALITIES AS a residual impact of your breakup, it is essential to practice the art of gratitude. Being grateful for little things is an important step in the grief process and will remind you to count your blessings however small they may be. You may be saying to yourself there is nothing to be grateful about because you are still dealing with lingering emotional pain from your breakup. However, if you choose to focus on negative details surrounding the breakup then this is where your energy will be directed. Wouldn't you rather direct this energy to more positive uses?

Practicing gratitude even while going through challenging situations can result in your happiness. The ability to show gratitude is your gift that can be used to encourage others and shift the focus away from your disappointments towards using your time and energy for uplifting others. What expressions of gratitude have you silently wrapped for others and yourself that you have not yet taken the time to hand over? While beating yourself up over a divorce, separation, sudden breakup, or any other adversity going on in your life, it is important to realize that the outlook you have of your future really depends on your attitude while going through personal trials. In Chapter 1 you were reminded that warriors stay in motion and develop support groups to receive training to keep motivated.

True, you may have endured terrible physical and financial losses, real hardships and unexpected setbacks. However, while it is normal to remember the hard times you've been through and how far you have come to improve your circumstances is healthy, this distinction between bad and good experiences must be made in your mind to lay the foundation for gratefulness. What are some of the things you can think of that you are grateful for? Is it your life, health, children, family, job, home, pet, career, spirituality, or inner peace? Make a list of things you are grateful for. Your gratitude checklist may also include being grateful for:

- Your resilience
- Kindness from others
- Emotional support

- Your freedom

Write these in your daily journal to keep a record of whatever your reasons are to be grateful. Acknowledging gratitude with gratitude enriches both yourself and the recipient. Reflecting on the reasons you should be thankful can help you to see there are more things to be grateful for when compared with those issues we are tempted to stress about.

Reflections

Within days of my breakup while on a solo trip, the breakup wounds were still fresh, and I was in tremendous emotional pain. I couldn't think of anything to be grateful for the first night of my vacation as I mustered up the courage to eat alone at dinnertime alongside couples on their honeymoons. As other diners feasted, waiters set place settings for a man they didn't know would not show up. It was after the first night I spent alone sobbing that I began to compile a gratitude list. After expressing my gratitude for life, for the beautiful ocean tumbling in the sand between my toes, and for even being healthy enough to enjoy a vacation, I began to think about the importance of my breakup in the grand scheme of things. The reminders of the little things brought me joy and peace. Then my perspective about gratitude began to shift.

Don't wait to be in a "good place" emotionally before making your gratitude checklist. Start your list with simple appreciations for people and other things you observe in your life that you should appreciate. Whatever it is you put on your gratitude checklist, it will put a smile on your face when you realize there is much to be thankful for.

Another way to show gratitude is to volunteer at a shelter or some other form of community service. Helping others will shift the focus from your problems and allow you to enjoy the immediate results from the positive impact you've made in the lives of others. These activities will help you recognize there is more to life than dwelling on the grief triggered by your ex. The more you give support to others, the more joy and accomplishment you will feel. In essence, when you practice showing gratitude, your outlook about other areas in your life gets better, stronger, and more positive. Remember the big things that impact your life but be appreciative for little things that teach you about yourself. This lesson I learned in the fall of 2015 when I had a strange epiphany.

As college midterms approached, I found myself reminiscing about the wonderful life I had while being married and the disaster of its ending all in that same year. I thought about the future and kept processing what was, how it unfolded, and what should have been over and over in my head. At the time, the pressures of college began to take last place in my mind, clouding my academic concentration. My grades began to suffer and so did my physical health. Feeling rather depressed over what I thought was a cloud of failure hovering over my personal life which cascaded into my academic performance, I confided in my college professor about my challenges.

My psychology professor was a brilliant man who went through many of life's stressful experiences and he was genuinely unafraid to share his wisdom with others. He was straightforward, unbiased, and at times unfiltered. The discussion I had with him about life and why I felt I was failing at everything was just the mental medicine I needed at the time. While this conversation did not win me any sympathy grades, it surely made me realize the importance of personal responsibility, accountability, and gratitude. I learned three valuable lessons after this conversation that changed the trajectory of my thinking.

Lesson 1: A failed marriage cannot constitute personal failure since a relationship involves two people. No matter how well you know a person, no single person can control their partner's mind to stay or leave a relationship. We don't even know the depth and capabilities of our own mind, so how can we predict all the capabilities in the mind of someone else? The people we love must be ready to speak and listen to resolve conflict. If they choose to flee from direct conversation and abandon the relationship, there is not much you can do since a relationship constitutes two people who must be willing to do the work.

This work in the relationship involves resolving

past and present conflicts, communication, and action steps necessary to resolve relationship disagreements. For this to work, both parties must be willing to make adjustments and paint a new picture in the relationship. Thus, as some would say, a person's life is like their own work or painting that started off as a blank sheet of paper and eventually got painted into their own shapes and colors that reflect their own character or experiences. Who are you to try to hold someone's paint brush to draw a painting of their life and how you think it should be?

You may rationalize that you want what's best for the person you love or think in retrospect years were spent in the long-term relationship with memories and many portraits together. However, the person who broke up with you chose to live their own life and paint their own portrait much like you are responsible for painting your own image of what you expect your life to be. So when a person suddenly ends a relationship with you, you may try to get them to change course, but it is really not up to you to change their mind about the path they chose to follow. Be grateful for the good and bad experiences in that relationship and what they taught you about yourself.

Lesson 2: If your failed relationship is causing you to fail at other things in your life, don't look at the situation as a loss. Look at failure as the price you paid for trying something new, for allowing you to love, and the catalyst pushing you in the direction you need to go.

> Reflections
>
> The reality for me was that I allowed challenges in my personal life to affect my academic performance and the grade I received was the price I paid for being capable of love. It was the price I chose at the time to pay whether I realized it or not.

Many successful people in business fail many times to succeed only once. Some may view their failures as underperformance, but those supposed failures are merely obstacles and necessary detours on the road to success. The sleepless nights and money some individuals lose in pursuit of success is the price they pay for the journey to their destination.

There are countless individuals in our society who have turned supposed failures into success stories. There are many public figures that now enjoy tremendous success but failed many times before succeeding. So, your broken relationship was not a failure, but it was a painful step on the road to get you closer to your own success. If you give up, you will never see what prize life had in store for you at the end of your detour.

Lesson 3: Our ability to change positively in response to what we perceive as failures is a sign of intelligence, not that of stupidity or defeat. Ignorance and failure are making their beds where you decide to lie down and give up. Where you will fail is the day you give up on yourself or fail to make changes in your life in response to the personal trial.

Be grateful for the experience of being able to show love. Be grateful for the setbacks and the little things that teach you to improve yourself. Be grateful to have a job to pay for your own bills and education. Be grateful for losing your job so you may be challenged to find a better one. Be grateful for the natural by-products of human existence whether these involve tragedies or triumphs. Be grateful for the good times spent with your former spouse. Be grateful you are alive and can rebuild whatever is broken.

At your funeral, college grades won't matter nor will material things, but it is the life you lived and those you positively impacted that will have lasting effects. Therefore, you must choose to focus on all the things you already have and not on what you've lost. Yes, learning gratitude is a choice! This positive thinking will send a message to the universe that you have learned the lesson of being grateful and you will receive more of the good things you already have.

Reflections

Armed with a new outlook about my failures, I immediately began to change my thinking. My new positive attitude permeated my life and led to a peaceful divorce with no need for lawyers and judicial intervention. Gratitude improved my physical and mental health. It made me stop to say thank you for the little things.

When you meditate on these three lessons and resolve to change your outlook about any perceived failures, your positive thinking will improve and become a beacon of light through life's toughest obstacles. As you become a humble student mastering the art of practicing gratitude, your mind will be prepared and become opened to forgiveness. Gratitude and forgiveness are choices you must make as they are woven together and fundamental to your personal happiness.

Four reminders to help you practice gratitude:

1. Practice gratitude by giving to others. Warriors stay in motion. Learn from your past or present warriors. Start writing down a daily gratitude checklist. Gratitude and giving to others leaves you open to forgiveness which are all linked to your personal happiness.
2. A failed relationship does not amount to personal failure because you cannot control your partner's mind. You cannot control how your ex decides to paint the next picture of their life. Be grateful for the lessons you've learned from the unfinished portrait you painted together before the breakup.
3. Your broken relationship was not a failure, but it was the price you paid during your journey on the road towards your own success.
4. Be grateful for the ability to adapt to change. Resistance to change and giving up is not an option.

JOURNAL COMMENTARY

Today I am grateful for

____

____

The phrases that resonated with me in this chapter

____

____

How do I feel inside when I show gratitude

____

____

Today I realize I can be successful if

____

____

Today I can learn valuable lessons from (name those influencers)

____

____

CHAPTER 7

LEARNING TO FORGIVE

Forgiveness is the key you turn to release your chains.

WHEN IT COMES TO FORGIVENESS for the people who've hurt us during our lifetime, the struggle to escape the devastating effects of the emotional wounds of abandonment can be very real and you may become a prisoner, branded by the stamp of lingering emotional pain from the abusive experience. The reality is, to forgive is to set free a prisoner from the chains of captivity and that prisoner is you. Is the ability to forgive your struggle? Are you shackled by grudges you accumulated from those who've caused you pain? Have you been convinced that the person who caused you pain is responsible for your decision to forgive? What is the delusion that you sold to yourself to make forgiveness seem impossible? What is the lie you sold to yourself over and over again that made you believe you cannot forgive and get past this obstacle?

Certainly, we are already free. There is no prisoner left to set free but our own self-limiting ideas telling us we need more components to be able to forgive. Those ingredients are already in the palm of your hands waiting for you to use them, urging you to freely forgive so you may watch your own magnificence grow.

THE ROOT OF FORGIVNESS

In Spring 2016, I watched a television program featuring many adult women who were abandoned when they were children growing up. Still hurt from being abandoned by their fathers when they were children, many women described the emptiness they felt after being deserted and how it affected them throughout their lives. Some had self-esteem issues, others overcompensated, lived promiscuous lives, and some were still looking for closure or even an apology from the offending parent years after the pain was inflicted on them. In essence, those women sought to fill a void left by the experience of abandonment and breaches of trust throughout their lives.

Some were still angry after many years of holding a grudge, others full of pain, but the common thread I noticed was almost all of them blamed the shortcomings of the parent for the bad choices they made in their own lives. In Chapter 4 we talked about shame, guilt, blaming others, and self-blame. In all of these self-limiting emotional reactions, we can conclude that these are not your weight to carry but your truth to accept. Accepting responsibility for the truth of your negative experiences is one of the most important steps of your journey on the path to healing.

Yes, forgiveness is linked to your healing. If a person does not heal pain from the past, they will not be able to forgive present pain perpetrated against them. Forgiveness certainly does not mean you must let the person who hurt you back into your life or miraculously forget the wrongs they've committed against you, but it involves you making the decision to release resentment and any animosity over the past suffering.

Forgiveness also involves releasing anger and any attempts to seek revenge. It is the deliberate action and conscious decision to accept the truth about your negative experiences and forgive yourself for the pain you feel inside because of it. These lessons I learned not as an adult, but as a child.

Like many people around the world, I grew up in a broken home. My parents divorced when I was very young and I had what was called an absentee father. In my mind, my father was not just an absentee person who contributed nothing to my upbringing, but a magician, appearing and disappearing from my childhood life only to return just to continue the cycle of abuse against my mother and by extension his children. I remember when I was very young, I pondered over my family dysfunction and analyzed my parents' life as well as the reasoning behind their fights. It seemed after all was said and done, the cycle of abuse I was observing was not what parenting should be like.

The disruption in my family unit growing up bothered me and I made the decision that the cycle of abuse I was witnessing at the time was not only unnecessary but should be terminated. While some may view bitter marital squabbles as unavoidable, adults should not underestimate a child's ability to convert the complexities of divorce to a simpler structure they can understand and recognize the forgiveness that has to occur to find some measure of internal happiness. After observing my environment, I longed for some adult to make the decision to peacefully end the cycle of abuse.

Therefore, when I was around eleven years old, my father called on the phone out of the blue expecting some sort of acknowledgment or consolation that he was still my father and I was still daddy's little girl. As we began to converse, it was as if he sensed my decision to end the cycle of abuse had already taken place. During that conversation, I informed my father that he was no longer allowed to be a magician in my life. He had not lived up to the true definition of what the role of a father should be and he was not allowed to manipulate my heart and mind into thinking that he was a role model anymore.

His place-keeping role as a father was relinquished by that little girl whether he wanted to end the cycle of abuse or not. That little girl held up a mirror to her father who could not stand the image staring back at him and who could not articulate any excuses for his behavior. After a moment of silence and still at a loss for words to defend his actions, he quietly hung up the phone, conceding to the truth he had just heard probably for the very first time in his life. That conversation would be the last one I had with my father.

From that moment onward, I forgave my parents for their shortcomings. I also forgave myself for putting up with their abuse and I did not pretend to have a perfect family or a father that was in my life as a protector anymore. I also decided from that day forward that the charade of hiding behind society's definition of a perfect family and the embarrassment of growing up without a father was not my burden to bear. It was my truth to accept.

I accepted that my parents were broken by their own pain that was beyond my ability to control or repair. I also accepted the fact that I was abandoned by a father who probably didn't even know how to be a parent or never accepted the responsibilities of being a parent. Whatever the case, the shame and worthlessness that came with growing up in a divorced household left with my father and I became more empowered to make my own decisions about life and my expectations from men.

My granny, the warrior, would make her appearance at various intervals in my life as I empowered myself to make my own decisions about my responses to those entering or leaving my life. That little girl's decision set the precedent for me to make timely decisions when I was abandoned after the sudden breakup of my marriage as an adult. Recognizing the truth about abandonment as a child and as an adult made me immediately understand I have the ability, at any given point in my life, to make the right choices and have rational discussions with the person causing me pain.

Which one of your warriors can you reference to help improve your understanding of abandonment? Understanding your emotions after your breakup will help you to avoid making reflex choices in reaction to the emotional pain that could become self-destructive. This understanding of emotional abandonment will also shield you from what I call "phantom void." That is, the feeling or illusion you impose on yourself to convince yourself that somehow your dysfunctional parents, your ex, or someone who may have hurt you, left you with an internal emptiness or emotional chasm you would not be able to fill.

Have you ever felt like someone caused something to go missing in your life that you can't quite seem to fix? If this feeling is left uncorrected, the void that you place upon yourself for the sins of other people is what will contribute to your self-imposed prison. A prison you must now free yourself from to be able to heal and forgive. Think back about the valuable lessons you've learned from your past regarding abandonment. Think about what you can learn from your warriors who've conquered the emotions you are struggling with. Those lessons at whatever age you receive your ah-hah moment will become your guiding compass. What has been your guiding compass to find forgiveness? Whenever I need guidance dealing with "phantom void" I think of the abbreviation C.F.R.

For me, C.F.R means: Cause,
Fault, and Responsibility.

CAUSE * FAULT = RESPONSIBILITY

In the real world, whoever caused the problem is usually responsible for fixing the issue. For example, in the case of a driving accident, if someone driving behind you rear-ended your brand-new vehicle, clearly that person would be responsible for fixing your car. You will more than likely have no problem getting the police report and insurance to support your claim to put blame where it belongs, on the negligent driver.

However, if that person rear-ended your vehicle, and fled the scene of the accident never to be seen or heard from again, that could complicate the situation. If the police respond to the scene of the accident only to find out the driver of the vehicle is a ghost, this can be problematic. If it is found the driver who is at fault and who caused the accident had no driver's license, the vehicle had no license plates, registration, or car insurance and the person cannot be found, you will have a decision to make. You may choose to stay at the scene of the accident indefinitely and wait for the driver to be honest and return to accept liability for the accident. Or you could accept responsibility for your own life and fix your vehicle so you do not continue to be inconvenienced by a situation beyond your control. Yes, it sucks, it will hurt, and it's not fair, nor is it justice you might think, but you may not get very far blaming someone who refuses to be present to acknowledge the damage they've caused.

CAUSE (You) * FAULT (You) =
RESPONSIBILITY (You)

If you continue to point fingers at the person you

believe caused the problems in your life and blame that person for your problems while holding them accountable for all their indiscretions, negligence, misconduct, lapses in judgement, dereliction, slip-ups, evil, loss of innocence, crimes, sins, transgressions, offenses, or misdeeds against you, then you will always believe it is the responsibility of someone else to fix your problems. In an illustrative sense, if you keep blaming others you are in essence standing indefinitely at the scene of the accident waiting for a ghost driver to return and apologize. Or you may decide to drive around with a damaged vehicle hoping for the ghost driver to eventually fix it.

While it's normal to acknowledge someone caused damage in your life, you have to decide if you will take control over your life to assume responsibility to fix the damage they created. You have the power to change the results of the inconvenience someone may have caused in your life. You have the power to adjust your reaction to an unavoidable situation. You have the power to take action. If you accept that you have the power to take responsibility for your own life, regardless of who caused the problem, the faster you will begin to make progress to become whole again. You should accept this responsibility because you don't deserve to live with the damage someone else caused in your life.

Since many of the problems in your life, including your breakup, are sometimes beyond your control, if you accept the responsibility for fixing these issues, it reduces the temptation to remain in the cycle of blaming others for the impact those negative experiences had on your life. Please recognize that while your environment may have affected you in a negative way, taking responsibility for the transgression of others does not make the person who caused you pain less accountable. It simply puts you in the driver's seat to fix your life instead of waiting for others to do it for you.

Similarly, if you hide your head in the sand and conclude it's no one's fault and take no action then that equation becomes:

CAUSE (0) * FAULT (0) = 0

That's right. Nothing happens. The unresolved issues remain unsolved indefinitely. Blaming others hinders you from making your own meaningful progress in life. There are some lessons you can learn about blame, sudden abandonment, and how this negative cycle undermines forgiveness.

LESSON 1: ACCEPT RESPONSIBILITY FOR YOUR OWN LIFE

- Even though it may be your parents', husband, wife, or some stranger who was the cause of your emotional pain, it is your responsibility to fill the void. It is your responsibility to fix the mess someone else caused so you can control the trajectory of your life. Waiting for a renegade parent or ex-spouse to offer an apology or fix the damage done to your life when they are unable to fix what is broken in their own life is like waiting for an elephant to fix a leaking faucet in your house. Or waiting for the ghost driver in the earlier illustration who damaged your new vehicle to show up and fix everything.

- You are the architect of your life and whatever is broken is your responsibility to fix. Forgiveness does not minimize what someone did to hurt you, it does not put you at fault for the problem nor does it mean you have to accept this person back into your life. Forgiveness comes from your heart after listening and learning from the whispers of gratitude. Forgiveness is acknowledging the faults of others and taking responsibility for fixing the negative impact they had on your life. This action will empower you to take control of your own life moving forward.

LESSON 2: STOP MAKING EXCUSES

- There are no excuses for abusing or suddenly abandoning another person after a breakup, nor are there any excuses for bad behavior in reaction to being abandoned. Never allow anyone, including your parents, spouse, or anyone else to justify any self-defeating behavior that will destroy your life. Both children and adults do have the ability to make the right choices in life even though they may have been exposed to bad parental role models.

While everyone reacts differently to emotional trauma, the "terrible teens" and "high-risk teenager" phases of growing up, or the "mid-life crisis" of adults, in response to family imbalances are times of turbulence you can choose to sidestep by taking action, reaching out for professional help, and avoiding the temptation of making excuses for your own bad behaviors.

LESSON 3: ABUSE CANNOT BE UNDONE. BUT CAN BE FORGIVEN

- If you were abandoned as an adult, this negative experience should not stop you from living your life in your way and on your terms. There is no undoing what was done to you. No make-up grades for the courses others allegedly made you fail. No one gets the chance to live yesterday over again. Today is a new day and this is your new life. What you endured, encountered, suffered, or confronted yesterday will not occur in the exact sequence again today. Each day is written in the present tense for you to do better and not in the past tense for you to stress about lost treasures. Your fight is not for the stale battles of yesterday but for today's and tomorrow's victories.

It's your choice to either remain a prisoner of your past or set yourself free to be the victor of your future. This is your now, and the time keeps counting whether you demand a do-over or not. You must simply forgive and move on towards better future performances. If you cannot learn forgiveness on your own, speak with a trusted friend or hire an expert to help you because there is just too much at stake. Your exclusive solo show is about to begin. Imagine you are already on stage and people paid for an expensive nonrefundable ticket to see you perform only once. There is no turning back, this is your stage and the universe is waiting for your performance. To perform at your best and to achieve your breakthrough, you must let go. In a very real way, forgiveness is a necessary component to finishing your purpose in life so you must overcome whatever void is eating away at your soul. Just like children are resilient, adults must test their resilience to emotional pain and forgive any betrayal, neglect, abuse, or other cruel acts you've endured so you can free the prisoner from emotional emptiness and bondage. That prisoner waiting to be set free is you. So accept responsibility for your own life and happiness. Take action, avoid excuses, heal yourself, and forgive.

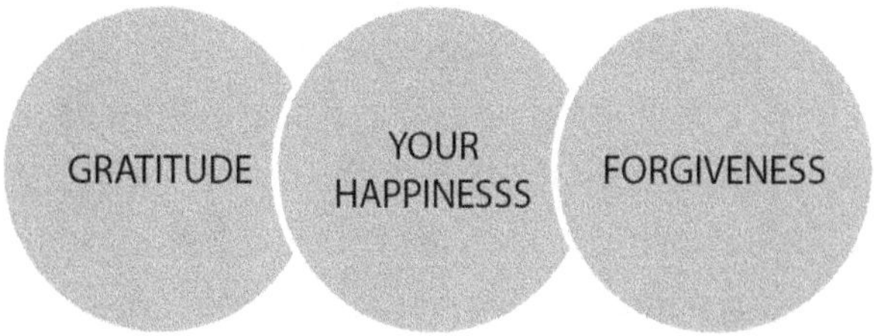

When you've unlocked the chains preventing you from learning gratitude and forgiveness, in the midst of this breakthrough, you will find a new key linked to your happiness.

Four reminders to help you learn to forgive:

1. Blame or resentment will shackle and hold you prisoner from the freedom of forgiveness.
2. Adult emotional pain can trigger feelings of abandonment you may have experienced in the past. Forgiveness is the truth you accept about your past and acknowledgment of the transgressions of others.
3. Accepting responsibility for your life does not change what someone did to hurt you, but it gives you power to change the trajectory of your life.
4. Stop making excuses for negative behaviors in response to the damage caused by another person. Abuse cannot be undone but can be forgiven.

JOURNAL COMMENTARY

Forgiveness is challenging because

The phrases that resonated with me in this chapter

Today I realize I need to forgive (list the names)

Today I can learn valuable lessons from

Today I accept responsibility for my life because (describe what's at stake)

CHAPTER 8

TAKE CONTROL OF YOUR LIFE

The brain is a powerful machine but fragile in the hands of its operator. Know that the way you drive this machine will determine your future.

SO FAR IN THIS JOURNEY to healing you've learned how to take control of multiple aspects of your life. You've received the tools required to help you unshackle obstacles that were holding you back from progressively restoring order in your life. If you are thinking the road to healing is too tough, think about the vehicle responsible for making all the changes in your life to orchestrate your successful recovery. Your brain is indeed this vehicle and it has untapped potential. Just when you think life has thrown you a trial you cannot handle, the brain steps up to show you that it is capable of handling any adversity if its driver is aware of when and how to make new turns.

Before finding my breakthrough after my breakup, I had to navigate many new turns in life. One of my new learning experiences is embedded in the portrait at the end of this chapter. The portrait reminds me of the brain's ability to take control in any chaotic situation and learn new skills to drive in a more positive direction. The portrait made me recall a very important experience that helped me take control of my life at a time when I thought it was spinning out of control. The story behind the portrait was another one of those "ah-ha" moments for me during my journey to heal from the effects of emotional abandonment after my breakup. My moment of transformation and embracing change came from learning how to draw.

You may be wondering, well, what does drawing have to do with abandonment, breakups, or all the emotional troubles and anxieties going on in your personal life? The truth is, learning new activities such as drawing may help you to see your problems from a different perspective.

Reflections

In 2018 during my junior year in college, still reeling from my divorce, I buried myself into the world of work and academic studying. However, I found myself buckling all over again under life's pressures and the demands of an engineering curriculum as if the wounds of the breakup had not yet healed. It felt like the same fear and self-destruction I faced in my freshman college years when the wounds of the breakup were still fresh. These feelings of failure that I thought were eradicated were actually resurfacing yet again. I thought my busy life would have made me "get over" that emotional challenge but those negative feelings of failure lingered. I felt like I was in a full-blown internal crisis all over again until I signed up for an art class that helped me develop the ability "to see." An art class helped me become confident enough to step outside of my comfort zone. I went from having no drawing talents whatsoever to drawing my portrait at the end of this chapter.

What's preventing you from taking control of your life? Are you stuck like I was in the mindset that trying a new skill is impossible? It's important to understand that it is not the act of drawing or learning a new skill that is difficult, but the skill of learning how "to see" a problem in a different way that is the challenge. Allowing yourself to be fluid enough to embrace change could be one of the keys to helping you achieve clarity. Since your upbringing, relationships, and your environment can shape the way you think, it is important to take steps to retrain your brain from one-way logical thinking to creative problem-solving.

Learning a new talent or skill can not only retrain your brain to think creatively instead of linearly, but may help you reach a different level of consciousness to solve complex issues in your life. Just like drawing is a discovery to see images and life experiences in a different way, so, too, we can discover different ways of seeing abandonment, breakups, emotional trauma, and various disappointments in life that could help us achieve inner peace.

Not only do you have the ability to control your inner peace but you can also use the logical left side of your brain to control your emotional right side and overcome lingering self-doubts after abandonment. Likewise, you can use the creative right side of your brain to develop new measures to overcome obstacles in your life in ways that the logical left would not be able to concoct. This control over your life can be accomplished in three steps.

STEP 1: LEARN NEW ACTIVITIES

Learning new activities allows your brain to embrace change. You will learn to enjoy your new freedom of not having to consult with anyone before making decisions. You can take on more challenges to propel your life in a direction that was once unthinkable when you were in a relationship. You will learn to never allow other people to place limitations upon you. When you step outside of your comfort zone beyond what you thought was your full potential, you may realize your true potential.

Reflections

The skill of using art to learn how to see did not come easily. On the first day of the art class, students were asked to draw a tree and animals made out of letters of the alphabet. Easy enough and quite trivial for college, I thought to myself at the time. However, to my surprise, I could draw a tree but wasn't able to digitally draw the animals from letters of the alphabet. The tree I drew on the first day of class would be the only art assignment I would be able to complete for weeks.

Perplexed and embarrassed, I approached the professor after almost one month of not completing any assignments, despite what I thought were my best efforts. On the brink of conceding to defeat and withdrawing from the art class, I told the professor I could not draw and maybe I was better off retreating to an engineering class where I felt more comfortable. To my surprise, he insisted that I had the ability to draw but just needed to find out what was preventing my ability "to see" and to translate my feelings into art. He also insisted that if I decided to stay in the class I must draw the portrait he selected. (Yes, the same portrait at the end of this chapter.) I chuckled to myself at his confidence in me that I had any shred of talent to draw that portrait.

I was thinking at the time either my professor or I was living in a twilight zone and my problem was not a "seeing" issue but I thought I simply had no drawing talents whatsoever. My professor also told me that I was the only engineering student in the class and most engineers usually lose patience and withdraw from the art class by the second week, so I should feel a sense of pride I lasted almost a month in the class. Far from feeling a sense of pride, I was feeling like a failure. After taking all the feedback from the professor I discovered he was right. My problem was not an emotional issue or anything to do with any physical inabilities, but it was an optical problem in the figurative sense. In essence, the act of drawing was not difficult, but my mindset was an obstacle. It was the skill of learning how to see things differently that shifted my mentality away from thoughts of drawing being too hard, which was the root of my artistic impotence.

Have you been postponing your goals and dreams to travel, dance, play an instrument, or learn a new language? Have you learned new construction skills to change a doorknob, lightbulb, or repair a faucet? Have you concluded learning a new skill is too hard? What have you accomplished that you never thought you were capable of? Warriors who have been through many battles are true fighters. They are constantly learning new facets of their skills and abilities. Have you discovered a new skill while exploring your independence from the responsibilities of being in a relationship? Did you wake up the warrior inside of you by rising to the challenge to rebuild your life? Have you started to listen to the voice inside you whenever it whispers, "You can do it?"

STEP 2: DECLUTTER

Take control of your life by decluttering your surroundings. You don't have to change everything and start with a clean slate, but whatever you want to change about your surroundings, know that you no longer need anyone's permission to make these changes. Stepping outside of your comfort zone not only involves giving yourself permission to make changes and trying new passions you've always had an interest in, but it also involves decluttering your mind.

Declutter your mind from your ex. Declutter your mind from the former vision you had in the old relationship with your partner. Declutter your mind from the self-limiting idea that the relationship failed because you were not good enough. You have nothing to prove to your ex but quite a bit to prove to yourself. Take note of what you're thinking. Remove unhealthy habits from your life and replace those with new healthy ones. Take an inventory of all the unfinished goals in your life and commit to accomplishing them one by one. Whether you have spiritual goals, health goals, skin goals, self-esteem goals, or new relationship goals, go after your goals with a vengeance.

STEP 3: REMEMBER YOU ARE NOT ALONE

There are many warriors who have been through breakups, and we all have the battle scars to prove it. Taking control of your life involves understanding that as bad as you may feel about your emotional progress to heal so far, you are not alone. One of the warriors from your past and in your present life knows what it feels like to go to bed alone and knows what solitude feels like. It will take time to feel like a warrior again. It will take time to feel like you have your life under control again. Healing does take time. Don't get discouraged.

Talking to others who have been through similar breakup experiences can be of great encouragement. As they share their stories of courage and struggles, take note of their strategies to navigate the challenging road to healing which allowed them to take control of their lives. You may be surprised to learn from other warriors who are currently in healthy relationships; they too went through the pain of a breakup at one point or another. Don't allow your breakup to break you or make you give up on your hidden talents.

You have the ability to choose multiple avenues of creative thinking to unleash your true potential instead of having your brilliance locked in a cage of self-doubt on the path of one-way thinking. What is preventing you from seeing creative solutions for your trials after your breakup? There is no need to fear going the distance in life alone or feel like you don't have talents to explore because some of the greatest triumphs and your untapped genius are waiting for you on the other side of fear. So regardless of what you have been through in life, remember:

- Never retreat and never surrender to failure.
- Fight to overcome your fears because your greatest achievements are waiting for you on the other side of fear.
- Never view anything as hard or difficult but surmountable.
- Embrace change and step outside of your comfort zone.
- Be open to feedback from others.
- Use both sides of your brain to find creative ways to solve your trials because you have unlimited potential and untapped creativity.
- Change your thinking and you will change your life.
- Change your thinking and you can achieve inner peace.
- You were designed for greatness.

WHAT ARE YOUR HIDDEN TALENTS?

Original Photo taken and illustrated by the author ©

Four reminders to help you take control of your life:

1. Feed your mind to access your untapped potential. Embrace change.
2. Learn new skills and activities to help you see your problems from a different perspective. Change your thinking and you can change your life.
3. Declutter your mind and your surroundings. Take an inventory of your unfinished goals and resolve to pursue each one with a vengeance.
4. Remember you are not alone and you were designed for greatness. Learn from the experience of other warriors who have battle scars.

JOURNAL COMMENTARY

Today I made a list of things that were unfinished in my life

___

___

The phrases that resonated with me in this chapter

___

___

Today I realize I have the potential to

___

___

Today I began to see my breakup in a different way because

___

___

Today I realize I was afraid of change because

___

___

CHAPTER 9

FINDING CLOSURE

Closure is you letting go of the old you.

IT WAS LIKE A SCENE out of a movie. The girl playfully straddled the driftwood close to the shore as the waves lapped against the sand, her teeth chattering from the warm water that suddenly turned cold. Gradually the buoyancy of the ocean carried her into deeper and deeper waters as her feet started lifting from the ocean floor. Panic set in as she propelled herself off the driftwood and frantically treaded water to safety. The driftwood was still within reach but what separated it and the girl were strong undercurrents in deep waters.

You may be thinking it would be foolish to blindly follow driftwood into unknown waters rather than stay in an area where you could quickly swim to safety, but tell that to a child who is inexperienced with the dangers of life. This story of a little girl was actually my story. It is my recollection of a frightening near-drowning experience I went through as a child that could have had a very different ending. This was one of many lessons life taught me about choices. It illustrates the serious decisions that must take place to choose to lose or win against life's challenges, to write your happy ending in your own way, on your own terms, and in your own personal storybook. Our own story and its ending are constantly being written whether we choose to write it or allow life's anxieties and abandonment experiences to write it for us.

Why do we follow life's driftwoods into dangerous waters and allow ourselves to sink into the undercurrents of unhappiness? Have you been reminiscing about why you were left behind by the person you thought loved you? Or have you been thinking about all the "what if's" of what your future would have been like, having children, growing old together, and sharing memories of all the happy times you shared? What driftwoods are you following into deeper waters? How much time have you allocated to following, sobbing, or reminiscing about a dead relationship that has already drifted off to sea?

While it is easier to answer these rhetorical questions as a back seat driver, when you are summoned by circumstances to control your life and when you are faced with your own challenges, how does your own self-investigation hold up under scrutiny? The reality is these forces of undercurrents in the illustrative story are the same ones working against you in your own life. So how do you find closure and avoid following driftwood only to be drowned in unhappy feelings and disquieting thoughts? To find closure you must first understand what closure means to you and then apply this definition to your own unique circumstances.

CLOSURE – WHAT IS IT?

Closure has different meanings for each person. Most psychological experts would agree in general terms that closure is knowing why you had a traumatic experience and recovering from the pain of that experience before moving on to better relationships. In other words, it involves not carrying emotional baggage from old relationships to new healthy relationships. This general view may be one perspective, but for those subjected to the brutality of a sudden breakup, knowing the reason a romantic relationship was terminated may not be a luxury you were privy to before, during, or after being discarded. So, if you are looking for someone else to give you closure or to articulate in a satisfactory way why they suddenly ended a long-term relationship with you, then you may never get the closure you are seeking. That is, until you learn to see closure differently.

Emotional abandonment after a sudden breakup opens the door to finding new ways to seek out closure besides getting answers and finding clarity from the person who caused the pain in the first place. Think about it, can you really find answers and happiness from the same person who initiated your unhappy experience in the first place? Can you really find closure from the same person and in the same way you lost it? Does that person have the level of consciousness required to remedy the problem? In retrospect, could anyone who inflicted the pain of abandonment on another person really offer any explanation sufficient to make up for all the damage done by their actions? What then does closure mean to you and what kind of closure are you seeking?

Trying to get answers to all the whys from the person who abandoned you can be likened to going to a dentist and demanding that he or she answer all the questions you need answers to for heart surgery! Would you really expect a dentist to provide satisfactory answers to all the questions you would have about the intricacies of heart surgery? Similarly, the person who abandoned you does not possess the expertise to fix your broken heart or give you all the answers about why they mistreated you.

Therefore, only you and you alone can perform the self-inspection needed to answer the foregoing series of rhetorical questions in this chapter written to speak directly to you. As mentioned in the previous chapter, learning new skills may help us embrace change and help our mind to see solutions to a problem creatively instead of linearly. Society trained us to think linearly like the storybook beginning, middle, and ending plot. Any interruption in this logical storybook plot tends to disrupt our entire way of thinking and throw our emotions into confusion. What we do need is creativity to think in a nonlinear way to be able to rewrite our own story when it gets interrupted.

While society is teaching you to think linearly, the world around you is constantly teaching you, if you are paying attention, to adapt to change. When you think about it, the universe with its planets and stars is in constant motion. Earth is in constant motion as well as the water cycle, atmosphere, trees, and animals are all undergoing constant change. Even the skin on your body is undergoing constant metamorphosis, shedding and creating new cells over and over again. Our body is engineered to adapt to change so, too, we must train our minds to adapt to change.

Hence, the world around us does not seek closure but always seeks acceptance, new mysteries, and beginnings. It does not really look for endings but is constantly working on reinventing. What then is preventing you from reinventing yourself? For me, it was this clarity that I could redevelop myself that gave me closure. Not the how and the mysteries of why I was discarded, but the clarity to accept that I can adapt to change and become bigger than the emotional mountains left behind after abandonment.

Therefore, closure is not something we are waiting

for someone to give us when they are good and ready years after they committed acts of injustice against us, but it is a gift we give to ourselves when others treated the gifts we gave to them with disrespect. Closure is a gift we already possess, waiting to be unleashed and its foundation is rooted in self-awareness. Therefore, closure is you letting go of the old you. You will get closure when you come to the understanding that you must accept the decisions of others (good or bad). You will also get closure when you come to the understanding that you already possess the gift to adapt to change and allow yourself to move forward with your life.

True, the heart may lag behind in accepting or understanding the closure process, but the heart is not the same as the brain. Most people would say, "Follow your heart," but in reality, the heart is always desperate and cannot be single-handedly trusted. Worst yet, after abuse and betrayal, the heart is very conflicted and is capable of deceiving even you after you've been backstabbed by those you trusted the most. You cannot rely on the heart to make decisions after being suddenly abandoned. It is the brain that reconciles acceptance and makes the final decision to move on and find closure.

Have you ever been on vacation in a beautiful place where you didn't want to leave? You could hear your desperate heart begging you to abandon everything and stay on that vacation permanently before the brain steps in and says, "Hello, you need money to stay on vacation forever. You have to get back to work next week, now get on that plane and go home!" Coming back from vacation to our opening illustrative story, it is the brain that makes the realization that staying and holding on to a "driftwood" relationship is pointless. It is the brain that calculates the risk to go after the dead relationship or to let go and swim safely to shore.

WHY IS CLOSURE SO CHALLENGING?

"I can't," "I am not," "But . . .but . . ." "I don't have . . ."

The first reason some may view closure as hard is because of their own self-limiting beliefs. Have you ever told yourself you can't do it on your own or can't live without the person who abandoned you? Or have you said, "I can't live alone, can't find closure until he or she apologizes for the pain they've caused?" If you are telling yourself you "can't" do something from your long list of "I can't," then these self-limiting words are actually at odds with your inherent power to make choices.

The person who left you exercised his or her power to choose to leave you. Why would you take away your own power by symbolically tying your hands behind your back with the words "I can't?" When this word gets beaten into your subconscious mind until it becomes a belief then those negative self-limiting thoughts will cripple you into thinking you don't have a choice but to be stuck with the cards life dealt.

I know what you are thinking. *'I can't' because I don't have the strength or experience to get closure on my own. 'I can't' because I am not a psychologist and don't have the time or money to allocate towards my own self-healing.* These excuses you sell to yourself can be extremely damaging when they leech into your identity as a person. If you identify yourself as a person who cannot do something by saying "I am not," then you will not do the work necessary to find your own closure. You put yourself at the mercy of your own self-limiting thinking that you do not have the power to change, heal, and grow. The truth is, we do have the ability to self-heal. Therefore, self-deception must be uprooted and banished from your thinking if you want to experience your true potential.

Look at that portrait again in Chapter 8. I mentioned before "I am not" an artist and "I could not" draw, only to learn to do the very things I told myself I couldn't do! You can learn to overcome the "I can't" and replace it with "I can" by learning to see yourself differently and finding more positive words to describe yourself. For example, compile a list of all your "I can't" and replace these with "I can."

NEGATIVE "I CAN'T"	**POSITIVE "I CAN"**
I can't swim.	I can learn how to swim.
I can't try new things alone.	I can learn to enjoy life with or without a significant other.
I can't draw.	I can learn how to draw and learn how to "see."
I can't love myself.	I can learn to love myself.
I can't be worthy of love.	I can learn to find my self-worth.

Once you begin to see that you are capable of self-healing, you will become bigger than the trial itself and recognize that you are good enough and qualified enough to successfully self-heal. Banish the inner voices that keep telling you there is no solution to your problem beyond what you can think of. Banish words like; "but," "never," "can't," from your vocabulary. Banish all those self-limiting tendencies that fight against you and that make finding closure seem difficult to accomplish. Do the work that you know is necessary to give up self-limiting tendencies and remove the power it exerts in your mind. Only you can give power to these self-limiting tendencies and only you can take its power away.

The second reason some may think getting closure is hard is because of fear. Warriors are sometimes afraid but they press on into battle anyway. Fear in the absence of action and courage leads to inactivity. Fear of the unknown paralyzes most people since they may find it hard to give up something tangible for something unseen. They can't envision life without being on the path that is familiar to them. To walk into a life of the unknown can be frightening for most. From being married to living the single life, from abundance to scarcity, from love to loneliness are all unknowns. To begin to overcome this fear of the unknown, you must speak the truth to yourself and trust the universe will fill the empty spot left in your life with abundance.

The third hijacker of closure is resentment. Yes, the resentment, anger, bitterness, and the blame you place on others and yourself. The "you did this to me" story we play over and over again. If you are filled with these self-limiting tendencies you will not find closure because these inclinations will be feasting upon your inner power like gangrene. Is this really what you want for yourself? To shrivel up and die inside because of the decisions of someone else? Do you really want to write the final chapter of your life out of revenge, anger, and resentment after allowing someone else to contribute to your failure to achieve your real purpose? I reckon this is not what you want for yourself! The people who do not come to the self-realization that they must let go of the driftwood of negative thinking are those who do not find closure.

HOW TO FIND CLOSURE

We've discussed banishing self-limiting beliefs, overcoming fear, and evicting anger, resentment, and other negative characteristics from your mind to find closure. Whether you were blindsided by your breakup, you didn't get answers to why the relationship crumbled, or you simply can't comprehend the unfolding of events because you believe you were the perfect couple together, it doesn't matter. What matters is you are where you are now and it is your responsibility to defeat those lingering self-limiting feelings. Write down all the things you learn about yourself through the experience and set new personal goals that require your drive and attention.

The ending of the relationship is really the beginning of your relationship with yourself. While you may be devastated you lost the partner you thought would have been there for you long-term, that person in your storybook may have very well been the savior who turned into a scoundrel in your very own movie plot. Whatever the case, the characteristics in the person who abruptly ended the relationship with you may be telling you they were not the person you painted them to be, so it's time to close the chapter and move on. Staying on the same page of the broken relationship does not change the characters in the plot. The story can change only when you turn the page and start writing a new plot with new characters and twists to create the ending you want for yourself.

By now, you should have come to realize that closure comes from you and is waiting for you to acknowledge its presence. There will be many chapters in your life, so it is important not to get stuck in your current one. You can rewrite your own plot and ending by changing your thinking. Focus on positive thoughts, maintain your sense of humor, and create beliefs that make you aware of the need to support this positive mental structure. Don't allow the blight of negative self-talk to rob you of the happiness and closure you deserve.

Write down all the self-limiting beliefs you have of yourself and write down all the positive beliefs in opposition to those self-sabotaging thoughts. What you will find after repeating positive things about yourself is that these thoughts become your reality. They become part of your new habits and positive character traits. The journey to closure requires courage to face your fears and conquer each of those fears step-by-step. Each page that you turn in your own storybook will allow you to let go of the old you to make way for the new you.

Four reminders to help you find closure:

1. You cannot really find answers from the person who caused your pain. You cannot find closure in the same way you lost it.
2. You will get closure when you come to an understanding that you already possess the gift to adapt to change and allow yourself to move forward with your life.
3. Banish negative words like "I can't," "I am not," "But," "I don't have." These words are obstacles to closure.
4. Closure is you letting go of the old you. To let go, you must turn the page in your own storybook and create new characters and plots to have the closure you want.

JOURNAL COMMENTARY

I realize the following driftwoods were in my life

____

____

The phrases that resonated with me in this chapter

____

____

Today I realize closure is attainable because

____

____

I realize these things were standing in the way of my closure

____

____

Today I let go of

____

____

CHAPTER 10

YOUR NARRATIVE TO LIVE YOUR BEST LIFE

Giving up is not one of the multiple-choice test selections in life, and neither is leaving a blank sheet.

THE PATH TO HEALING FROM a sudden breakup was quite a journey! You have gone through an odyssey from the initial shock after the breakup, anger, denial, blame, healing from emotional, spiritual, and financial loss, then learned the power of gratitude, forgiveness, and closure. Are you now ready to live your best life? Do you have the courage needed to write the next chapter?

It takes courage not to abandon unfinished dreams in your life. It takes courage to not give up and keep persisting. It takes courage to look in the mirror to make internal changes and realign the rest of your life towards the path of success. It takes courage to be disciplined with your finances, feelings, your children, family, your ex, your employer, your emotions, mind, body, soul, and in every aspect of your life. If you have the courage to stay on course, you will live to see only an obscure vision of those who have hurt you far in the distance in your rearview mirror, while your road ahead will become clearer and clearer.

It takes courage to recognize when a person who mistreated you and departed from your life, simply does just that —leave. They leave you with your own capacity to love that they initially met you with and the power to choose who to entrust that love to going forward into the future. You may think that love is gone with this person that broke up with you, but love is still with you. If you feel like you have overextended all the love you have to the old relationship and your ex left with all of your love, then you must recognize you have the power to mint more because your capacity to love is limitless.

Love for yourself gave you the courage to find closure and love for yourself will help you write your narrative to live your best life. To write a better story for yourself you must develop boundaries from now on and choose who you will or will not have in your life. Once you find closure and set those boundaries, hold fast to your decision. You've done the work to heal yourself and deserve to have only positive people in your life that will reinforce all the things you've accomplished to be a better person. Once you become the best version of yourself, you will know who you are, what makes you tick, and what empowers you. You get to decide when you will or will not start dating again. You also get to decide how you will achieve living the life you intend to live.

The five steps to living your best life requires:

1. Focus. Concentrate on what you want and what you would like to achieve. If you want to earn a degree, focus on getting a degree. When you are focused on what you want you will live a life of purpose and intent. Are there dormant talents you've always wanted to pursue? If so, focus on those talents one by one. Maybe you've always wanted to learn to drive, swim, paint, dance, cook, volunteer, or start your own business. Whatever it is you set your mind to achieve, focus on achieving that goal.
2. Taking action. If you do nothing to live your best life, guess what? You will not live your best life. Take responsibility for your life. Live each day with your mission clearly in mind and never leave a blank sheet in your storybook. Maybe you can think back in your life to when you were younger, five years ago, or maybe ten years ago. Time did not wait for you to take action. If you did not take action to finish the mission you had ten years ago, that mission would still remain a blank sheet. Whatever goal you set to accomplish, take action to get it done and mark the task complete.
3. Journaling. You started a journal at the beginning of this book and will need

to keep one for the rest of your successful journey beyond healing. Your journal will manage your thoughts for you, it will be your sounding board to vent to, and it will be your cheerleader to record and celebrate your new experiences, or breakthroughs. When you look back at your journal, it will show you how far you've come and the distance you have left to achieve your goals. The power of writing down your thoughts forces the universe to make those thoughts your reality.

4. Loving you. To live your best life is to love yourself and others. Take care of your mind, body, and spirit. You will receive many forms of criticism, even from yourself, as you work towards your goals. Silence your inner critic and banish self-limiting words. Remove bad habits and don't engage in any activity that will sabotage what you have accomplished. You've done the work, you learned to be disciplined with your self-care regimen, you are worthy of living your best life, and you are capable of reaching the goal of living your best life.
5. Setting goals and visualization. Set goals aligned with your mission. Set long-term, short-term, daily, weekly, monthly, and annual goals. Visualize yourself accomplishing those goals until the picture is cemented in your

> mind. When you can visualize your goals, dream them, believe them, take action, and talk about them like they have already been achieved. Then, they will one day materialize into reality.

These five steps to living your best life are doable and within your grasp. Reach for it. Fight for it. Tap into your inner warrior and let this become your agent of transformation. I believe in you. Now you must believe in yourself. I believe there is a warrior within you, and I'm sure you can hardly wait to meet the new you.

Four reminders to help you live your best life:

1. Be courageous enough to live your best life.
2. Focus on what you want, your goals, mission, and purpose.
3. Keep your journal to manage your thoughts and track your progress.
4. Love yourself and others. Set goals and visualize these goals as already accomplished.

JOURNAL COMMENTARY

Today I am willing to employ more courage in my approach to

The phrases that resonated with me in this chapter

Today I realize my mission and purpose is to

I congratulate myself for being able to

Today, I can recognize disorder in my life, I feel loved, and I am empowered to achieve anything.

What choice will you make today to rewrite the ending of your story?

Final Reflections

By now, you should have experienced one or multiple breakthroughs. You must realize you broke up, but you are not broken. You have a purpose and great capacity to love if you can make the connection. Love is kindness and resilience. It is watching your words and actions, helping others live instead of taking a life. Love is you. Love is me and the ability to see the needs of others without passing judgment. Love is looking in the mirror life handed to us to change to old habits that are hurting us and those we interact with. It is who we are inside, not our harsh opinions of others. Love is remembering how we were as children, innocent, free like butterflies in a bamboo patch. Love is learning patience, compassion, and self-sacrifice. It is endurance through tough times and always learning what makes us culturally different yet similar in every way. It is having the last say in the final chapter of your life and writing your story in your own way. Love is forgiveness, gratitude, and learning when to let go. Through this breakup and many experiences, I discovered love is your canvas. I hope this book helped you find your breakthrough to become the warrior that you didn't know was inside you. Today is your rebirth. Today you will rise from the ashes of your past to start a new life fueled with fire and passion to achieve a brighter future. I hope you are more empowered to turn the page in this chapter of your life, undaunted by your trials and negative experiences. Today you decide to make what seems impossible, attainable. As Granny would say, "Don't let disappointments in life reduce you to ruin, don't worry about anything. Go, you will do good."

EXCERPT FROM UPCOMING BOOK:

EMPOWER THE WARRIOR WITHIN

How to Stand Up to Bullies in the Workplace

Vanessa Goans

INTRODUCTION

TODAY WE ARE CONFRONTED WITH the reality of bullies on the playground and in the workplace. Bullying has become part of a wider conversation today to raise awareness about the disastrous effects this abuse has on children. However, the response may be quite different when adult bullying is reported. Most of us would like to believe childhood behaviors vanish naturally when people mature, but sadly adults can be bullies just like children.

Many studies have described bullying as a form of psychological abuse. A bully is a person who carries out repeated and sustained abuse against another person, and when the bully recruits others to join in the attacks, this can be described as mobbing. Adult bullying and mobbing are serious problems facing adults in the workplace resulting in talent flights, staff turnovers, loss in productivity, increases in health costs, and other issues for employers and employees.

This was my dilemma when I faced my workplace bully and was unprepared for the backlash that radiated from the experience. I was at the peak of my career working fulltime, on full scholarship in engineering school, and picking at the fresh wounds of a painful divorce. Though there were many hurricane events going on in my personal life at the time, I was still thriving. I worked harder, overcompensated by taking on additional assignments at work, and as some would say, I was "firing on all cylinders." My competence, resilience, drive, and momentum towards success didn't go unnoticed. It seemed to be one of the catalysts behind the air strikes from a general manager who applied pressure to make me quit on the road to success. To achieve his agenda, he began an extensive bullying campaign to derail my reputation and my career advancements.

I became the target of harsh criticism, negative rumors, damaging performance reviews, and other unsubstantiated allegations as my bully enlisted supporters to instigate a full smear campaign against my reputation. Former allies scattered and became distant to protect their own careers from being tarnished, and

I became socially isolated in the workplace. Since this bully had a superior leadership position, his accusations were accepted as gospel without examination of facts.

The avalanche of damage was inescapable. He made sure I suffered emotionally and financially, which led me to take action to defend my reputation. Additionally, his misogynistic bullying campaign ensured my stellar reputation for high performance did not see daylight for many years. In the thick of the attacks, which mushroomed into multiple bullies, I called out sick for the first time in over nine years to preserve my mental health. With no support from all the internal company agencies that were supposed to uphold fairness and inclusivity, I found myself on the brink of losing my job just because a bully felt it should be so. Some would say, "Get thicker skin," "Get over it," or "Just ignore the bully," but too often those words are ineffective when confronted with a bully in the workplace.

Dealing with an adult bully is an intricate situation. If you ignore the bully and do nothing, you may appear intimidated or afraid. If you do respond to the bully, your entire defense may be twisted to make you look like the problem. If the bully successfully paints you as the problem, it may be easier for the company to get behind the bully, tolerate the problem, or misunderstand the conflict. Once you become labelled as the problem, or the "black sheep," the company may view you as a dispensable liability who would be a good candidate for termination. From my personal experience, it is very difficult, if not impossible, to reason with an adult bully so it's often best not to suffer in silence. Get supporters and make the choice not to become a victim.

Bullies attack their targets due to their own personal insecurities and desire for power or control. Usually their targets include talented, well-educated, knowledgeable, productive, and competent individuals with all the positive attributes needed by the employer. These are hardly the traits of a victim. However, your bully is infuriated by your talents, independent ideas, and views these positive traits or your differences as a threat. As a result, the bully creates a toxic work environment to upend your career in hopes that you will become ineffective at your job, develop health issues, or quit altogether.

Not only can bullying have devastating effects on your physical and mental health, but the stress from the attacks of a bully may also lead to anxiety and depression. It was especially difficult for me to process the subtlety of bullying when I, a person of color, experienced bullying under the thumb of a person of color who should have known what oppression feels like. This adds another layer to adult bullying which may be misunderstood or overlooked when the target attempts to get help to eliminate the attacks.

In reality, bullies will come into your life packaged

in all forms of camouflage regardless of culture, gender, race, or country. In this modern time no one, child or adult, deserves to be bullied. So, if you are experiencing career sabotage fueled by the abuse of a bully in the workplace, by standing up, summoning your inner warrior, and taking action, you will send a clear message that your answer to bullying is NO.

ABOUT THE AUTHOR

Vanessa is an author, inventor, and electrical engineer. Through her works as an author, she seeks to encourage people who have gone through harrowing life experiences such as: failed relationships, unanticipated abandonment in marriages, and painful breakups. Her goal is to empower those who are on the verge of giving up on life and on themselves as a result of these unpleasant life experiences. By sharing her own compelling story, her mission is to help people get the healing they deserve, attain their highest potential, and write their own narrative to achieve their greatest breakthrough. She lives in New York City, and when not writing, she enjoys dancing, traveling, and bringing new invention ideas to life.

TESTIMONIALS

"Divorce is a life-changing setback that could lead to discouragement and negative thinking. Empower the Warrior Within shows you how you can navigate the emotional pain from a breakup and turn this bad experience into powerful tools for success. Vanessa does a brilliant job teaching us how to turn adversity into greatness."

—Jack Canfield, Coauthor of the *Chicken Soup for the Soul®* series and *The Success Principles. How to Get from Where You Are to Where You Want To Be™*.

"After a bone breaks and heals, it's stronger than a bone that has never been through a trauma. *Empower the Warrior Within* applies these same principles to daily life. When we are broken physically, emotionally, or financially, we can also come back stronger than before. Vanessa does a magnificent job of teaching us how to use the bricks thrown at us in life to build a stronger foundation."

—Dr. David Friedman,
TV and Radio Talk Show Host,
Award-Winning, #1 best-selling
author of *Food Sanity*.

"Vanessa has done a great job of helping people to understand the pain of losing a loved one via breakup. Her book offers tremendous hope, encouragement, and empowerment to people who suffer loss. She takes you on a powerful journey of surviving the emotional turmoil and regaining your strength back to be yourself again. Must read!"

—Zeena Marshall M.D

"Divorce is a setback like no other in life. If you don't empower yourself with positivity, then negativity can set it. In *Empower the Warrior Within* Vanessa shows how to bounce back with positivity and get your life back. Her book empowered me to do the inner work of forgiveness after my divorce. That has helped me get on with my life."

—Harris Jensen, MD
Psychiatrist
Author of Prescription for Positivity

LET'S STAY IN TOUCH

For more information about the author visit:

www.VanessaGoans.com

- You'll receive a free gift.
- You'll be the first to know about any upcoming virtual presentations, group coaching, and training workshops.

If this book helped you any way, please reach out and let me know. I look forward to hearing from you.

CPSIA information can be obtained
at www.ICGtesting.com
Printed in the USA
BVHW071601081121
621076BV00006B/225

9 781737 652205